D0358027

≡ *Fast Talk*

French

Guaranteed to get you talking

Contents

⇒ Special Features

Before You Go

Many visitors to France get around without speaking a word of French, but just a few phrases go a long way in making friends, inviting service with a smile, and ensuring a rich and rewarding travel experience – you could discover a cosy vineyard off the tourist track, experience a sublime meal, or grab that great shopping bargain.

PRONUNCIATION TIPS

The sounds of French can almost all be found in English, and if you read our coloured pronunciation guides as if they were English you'll be understood.

★ The few sounds that do differ from English include the throaty r (a bit like a growl) and ew (said as the 'ee' in 'see' with rounded lips). Note also that zh is pronounced as the 's' in 'pleasure'.

★ French has nasal vowels (pronounced as if you're trying to force the sound 'through the nose'). English is similar to some extent – eg when you say 'sing', the 'i' is nasalised

by the 'ng'. We've used nasal consonant sounds (m, n, ng) after the nasal vowel so you can produce the sound with confidence.

★ Syllables in French are, for the most part, equally stressed – as English speakers tend to stress the first syllable, try adding a light stress on the final syllable of French words to compensate.

MUST-KNOW GRAMMAR

The structure of French holds no major surprises for English speakers since the two languages are quite closely related.

★ French has a formal and informal word for 'you' (*vous* voo and *tu* tew respectively). When talking to someone familiar or younger than you, use the *tu* form. Phrases in this book use the form that is appropriate to the situation. Where both forms can be used, they are indicated by pol and inf respectively.

★ French has masculine and feminine forms of words, eg *beau/belle* bo/bel (beautiful), indicated in this book by m and f respectively.

★ Verbs have a different ending for each person, like the English 'I do' vs 'he/she do**es**'. You'll still be understood if you use the dictionary form of a verb in all contexts.

SOUNDS FAMILIAR?

Many French words are part of the English vocabulary – thanks to the Norman invasion of England in the 11th century, some estimate that three-fifths of everyday English vocabulary arrived via French. You'll recognise *café*, *déjà vu*, *rendez-vous*, *cliché* …

Fast Talk French

Don't worry if you've never learnt French (*français* fron·say) before – it's all about confidence. You don't need to memorise endless grammatical details or long lists of vocabulary – you just need to start speaking. You have nothing to lose and everything to gain when the locals hear you making an effort. And remember that body language and a sense of humour have a role to play in every culture.

"you just need to start speaking"

Even if you use the very basics, such as greetings and civilities, your travel experience will be the better for it. Once you start, you'll be amazed how many prompts you'll get to help you build on those first words. You'll hear people speaking, pick up sounds and expressions from the locals, catch a word or two that you know from TV already, see something on a billboard – all these things help to build your understanding.

5

5. Phrases to Learn Before You Go

What are the opening hours?

Quelles sont les heures d'ouverture?

kel zon lay zer doo·vair·tewr

French business hours are governed by a maze of regulations, so it's a good idea to check before you make plans.

I'd like the set menu, please.

Je voudrais le menu, s'il vous plait.

zher voo·dray ler mer·new seel voo play

The best-value dining in France is the two- or three-course meal at a fixed price. Most restaurants have one on the chalkboard.

Which wine would you recommend?

Quel vin vous conseillez? kel vun voo kon·say·yay

Who better to ask for advice on wine than the French?

Can I address you with 'tu'?

Est-ce que je peux vous tutoyer?

es·ker zher per voo tew·twa·yay

Before you start addressing someone with the informal 'you' form, it's polite to ask permission first.

Do you have plans for tonight?

Vous avez prévu quelque chose ce soir?

voo za·vay pray·vew kel·ker shoz ser swar

To arrange to meet up without sounding pushy, ask friends if they're available rather than inviting them directly.

10. Phrases to Sound Like a Local

Cool!	**Génial!**	zhay·nyal
No worries.	**Pas de soucis.**	pa der soo·see
Sure.	**D'accord.**	da·kor
No way!	**Pas question!**	pa kay·styon
Just joking!	**Je plaisante!**	zher play·zont
Too bad.	**Tant pis.**	tom pee
What a shame.	**Quel dommage.**	kel do·mazh
What's up?	**Qu'est-ce qu'il y a?**	kes keel ya
Well done!	**Bien joué!**	byun zhoo·ay
Not bad.	**Pas mal.**	pa mal

10. Phrases to Start a Sentence

When is (the tour)?	C'est quand (l'excursion)? say kon (leks·kewr·syon)
Where is (the station)?	Où est (la gare)? oo·ay (la gar)
Where can I (buy a ticket)?	Où peut-on (acheter un billet)? oo per·ton (ash·tay um bee·yay)
Do you have (a map)?	Avez-vous (une carte)? a·vay·voo (ewn kart)
Is there (a toilet)?	Y a-t-il (des toilettes)? ya·teel (day twa·let)
I'd like (a coffee).	Je voudrais (un café). zher voo·dray (ung ka·fay)
I'd like to (return this).	Je voudrais (rapporter ceci). zher voo·dray (ra·por·tay ser·see)
Can I (enter)?	Puis-je (entrer)? pweezh (on·tray)
Do I have to (book a seat)?	Faut-il (réserver une place)? fo·teel (ray·zair·vay ewn plas)
Can you (write down the price)?	Pouvez-vous (écrire le prix)? poo·vay voo (ay·kreer ler pree)

Chatting & Basics

≡ Fast Phrases

Hello./Goodbye.	Bonjour./Au revoir.
	bon·zhoor/o rer·vwar
Please./Thank you.	S'il vous plaît./Merci.
	seel voo play/mair·see
Do you speak English?	Parlez-vous anglais?
	par·lay·voo ong·glay

Essentials

Yes.	Oui.
	wee
No.	Non.
	non
Please.	S'il vous plaît.
	seel voo play
Thank you (very much).	Merci (beaucoup).
	mair·see (bo·koo)
You're welcome.	Je vous en prie.
	zher voo zon·pree
Excuse me.	Excusez-moi.
	ek·skew·zay·mwa
Sorry.	Pardon.
	par·don

9

Language Difficulties

Do you speak English?	Parlez-vous anglais? par·lay·voo ong·glay
Does anyone speak English?	Y a-t-il quelqu'un qui parle anglais? ya·teel kel·kung kee par long·glay
Do you understand?	Comprenez-vous? kom·prer·nay·voo
I understand.	Je comprends. zher kom·pron
I don't understand.	Je ne comprends pas. zher ner kom·pron pa
I speak a little.	Je parle un peu. zher parl um per
What does ... mean?	Que veut dire ...? ker ver deer ...
How do you pronounce this?	Comment le prononcez-vous? ko·mon ler pro·non·say voo
How do you write ...?	Comment est-ce qu'on écrit ...? ko·mon es kon ay·kree ...
Could you please repeat that?	Pourriez-vous répéter, s'il vous plaît? poo·ree·yay voo ray·pay·tay seel voo play
Could you please write it down?	Pourriez-vous l'écrire, s'il vous plaît? poo·ree·yay voo lay·kreer seel voo play

Could you please speak more slowly?	Pourriez-vous parler plus lentement, s'il vous plaît? poo·ree·yay voo par·lay plew lon·ter·mon seel voo play
Slowly, please!	Lentement, s'il vous plaît! lon·ter·mon seel voo play

Greetings

Hello.	Bonjour. bon·zhoor
Hi.	Salut. sa·lew
Good morning/afternoon.	Bonjour. bon·zhoor
Good evening/night.	Bonsoir. bon·swar
See you later.	À bientôt. a byun·to
Goodbye.	Au revoir. o rer·vwar
How are you?	Comment allez-vous? pol ko·mon ta·lay·voo Ça va? inf sa va

Fast Talk   Greetings

A kiss on each cheek remains a common greeting in France, though between men (and when meeting a man or a woman for the first time) a handshake is more usual.

Fine, thanks. And you?	Bien, merci. Et vous/toi? pol/inf
	byun mair·see
	ay voo/twa

Titles

Mr	Monsieur (M)
	mer·syer
Ms/Mrs	Madame (Mme)
	ma·dam
Miss	Mademoiselle (Mlle)
	mad·mwa·zel

Introductions

What's your name?	Comment vous appelez-vous? pol
	ko·mon voo za·play·voo
	Comment tu t'appelles? inf
	ko·mon tew ta·pel
My name is ...	Je m'appelle ...
	zher ma·pel ...
I'm pleased to meet you.	Enchanté(e). m/f
	on·shon·tay
It's been great meeting you.	Ravi d'avoir fait ta connaissance. inf
	ra·vee da·vwar fay ta ko·nay·sons
I'd like to introduce you to ...	Je vous présente ...
	zher voo pray·zont ...
✂ This is ...	Voici ...
	vwa·see ...

PHRASE BUILDER

This is my ...	Voici mon/ma ... m/f	vwa·see mon/ma ...
child	enfant	on·fon
colleague	collègue	ko·leg
friend	ami(e) m/f	a·mee
husband	mari m	ma·ree
partner	partenaire	par·ter·nair
wife	femme f	fam

What's your ...?

Quel est votre ... ? pol
kel ay vo·trer ...
Quel est ton ...? inf
kel ay ton ...

PHRASE BUILDER

Here's my ...	Voici mon ...	vwa·see mon ...
address	adresse	a·dres
email	e·mail	ay·mel
mobile number	numéro de portable	new·may·ro der por·ta·bler
phone number	numéro de téléphone	new·may·ro der tay·lay·fon

Personal Details

Where are you from?

Vous venez d'où? pol
voo ver·nay doo
Tu viens d'où? inf
tew vyun doo

13

PHRASE BUILDER

I'm from ...	Je viens ...	zher vyun ...
Australia	d'Australie	dos·tra·lee
Canada	du Canada	dew ka·na·da
England	d'Angleterre	dong·gle·tair
New Zealand	de la Nouvelle-Zélande	der la noo·vel·zay·lond
the USA	des USA	day zew·es·a

Are you married?	Est-ce que vous êtes marié(e)? m/f pol es·ker voo zet mar·yay Est-ce que tu es marié(e)? m/f inf es·ker tew ay mar·yay
I'm single.	Je suis célibataire. zher swee say·lee·ba·tair
I'm married.	Je suis marié(e). m/f zher swee mar·yay
I'm separated.	Je suis séparé(e). m/f zher swee say·pa·ray

Age

How old are you?	Quel âge avez-vous? pol kel azh a·vay·voo Quel âge as-tu? inf kel azh a·tew
I'm ... years old.	J'ai ... ans. zhay ... on
How old is your son/daughter?	Quel âge a votre fils/fille? kel azh a vo·trer fees/fee·yer
He/She is ... years old.	Il/Elle a ... ans. eel/el a ... on

Occupations & Study

What's your occupation?	Vous faites quoi comme métier? pol voo fet kwa kom may·tyay Tu fais quoi comme métier? inf tew fay kwa kom may·tyay
I'm an office worker.	Je suis un(e) employé(e) de bureau. m/f zher swee zun/zewn om·plwa·yay der bew·ro
I work in (education).	Je travaille dans (l'enseignement). zher tra·vai don (lon·sen·yer·mon)

PHRASE BUILDER

I'm (a) ...	Je suis (un/une) ... m/f	zher swee zun/zewn ...
retired	retraité(e) m/f	rer·tray·tay
self- employed	indépendant(e) m/f	un·day·pon·don(t)
student	étudiant(e) m/f	ay·tew·dyon(t)
unemployed	chômeur m	sho·mer
	chômeuse f	sho·merz

What are you studying?	Que faites-vous comme études? pol ker fet·voo kom ay·tewd Que fais-tu comme études? inf ker fay·tew kom ay·tewd
I'm studying engineering.	Je fais des études d'ingénieur. zher fay day zay·tewd dun·zhay·nyer
I'm studying French.	Je fais des études de français. zher fay day zay·tewd der fron·say

Interests

What do you do in your spare time?	Que fais-tu pendant tes loisirs? ker fay·tew pon·don tay lwa·zeer
Do you like (art)?	Aimes-tu (l'art)? em·tew (lar)
Do you like (sport)?	Aimes-tu (le sport)? em·tew (ler spor)
I like (music).	J'aime (la musique). zhem (la mew·zeek)
I like (movies).	J'aime (les films). zhem (lay feelm)
I don't like (cooking).	Je n'aime pas (cuisiner). zher nem pa (kwee·zee·nay)
I don't like (hiking).	Je n'aime pas (la randonnée). zher nem pa (la ron·do·nay)

Feelings

Are you (cold)?	Avez-vous (froid)? pol a·vay voo (frwa) As-tu (froid)? inf a·tew (frwa)
I'm (hot).	J'ai (chaud). zhay (sho)
I'm not (hungry).	Je n'ai pas (faim). zher nay pa (fum)
I'm not (thirsty).	Je n'ai pas (soif). zher nay pa (swaf)

Are you ...?	Êtes-vous ...? pol	et voo ...
	Es-tu ...? inf	ay·tew ...
I'm ...	Je suis ...	zher swee ...

PHRASE BUILDER

I'm not ...	Je ne suis pas ...	zher ner swee pa ...
happy	heureux m	er·reu
	heureuse f	er·reuz
in a hurry	pressé(e) m/f	pray·say
sad	triste	treest
tired	fatigué(e) m/f	fa·tee·gay
well	bien	byun

Numbers

0	zéro	zay·ro
1	un	un
2	deux	der
3	trois	trwa
4	quatre	ka·trer
5	cinq	sungk
6	six	sees
7	sept	set
8	huit	weet
9	neuf	nerf
10	dix	dees
11	onze	onz

12	douze	dooz
13	treize	trez
14	quatorze	ka·torz
15	quinze	kunz
16	seize	sez
17	dix-sept	dee·set
18	dix-huit	dee·zweet
19	dix-neuf	deez·nerf
20	vingt	vung
21	vingt et un	vung tay un
22	vingt-deux	vung·der
30	trente	tront
40	quarante	ka·ront
50	cinquante	sung·kont
60	soixante	swa·sont
70	soixante-dix	swa·son·dees
80	quatre-vingts	ka·trer·vung
90	quatre-vingt-dix	ka·trer·vung·dees
100	cent	son
1000	mille	meel
1,000,000	un million	um meel·yon

Fast Talk · **Telling the Time**

The 24-hour clock is commonly used when telling the time in French. After the half hour, use the next hour minus (*moins* mwun) the minutes until that hour arrives, eg '20 to seven' is *Il est sept heures moins vingt* ee lay set er mwun vung.

Time

What time is it?	Quelle heure est-il?	kel er ay·teel
It's one o'clock.	Il est une heure.	ee·lay ewn er
It's (10) o'clock.	Il est (dix) heures.	ee·lay (deez) er
Quarter past (one).	Il est (une) heure et quart.	ee·lay (ewn) er ay kar
Half past (one).	Il est (une) heure et demie.	ee·lay (ewn) er ay der·mee
Quarter to (one).	Il est (une) heure moins le quart.	ee·lay (ewn) er mwun ler kar
At what time?	À quelle heure?	a kel er
At ...	À ...	a ...
in the morning	du matin	dew ma·tun
in the afternoon	de l'après-midi	der la·pray·mee·dee
in the evening	du soir	dew swar

Days

Monday	lundi m	lun·dee
Tuesday	mardi m	mar·dee
Wednesday	mercredi m	mair·krer·dee
Thursday	jeudi m	zher·dee
Friday	vendredi m	von·drer·dee

Saturday	samedi m	sam·dee
Sunday	dimanche m	dee·monsh

Months

January	janvier m	zhon·vyay
February	février m	fayv·ryay
March	mars m	mars
April	avril m	a·vreel
May	mai m	may
June	juin m	zhwun
July	juillet m	zhwee·yay
August	août m	oot
September	septembre m	sep·tom·brer
October	octobre m	ok·to·brer
November	novembre m	no·vom·brer
December	décembre m	day·som·brer

Fast Talk Starting Off

When starting to speak another language, your biggest hurdle is saying aloud what may seem to be just a bunch of sounds. The best way to do this is to memorise a few key words, like 'hello', 'thank you' and 'how much?', plus at least one phrase that's not essential, eg 'how are you', 'see you later' or 'it's very cold/hot' (people love to talk about the weather!). This will enable you to make contact with the locals, and when you get a reply and a smile, it'll also boost your confidence.

Dates

What date?	Quelle date? kel dat
What's today's date?	C'est quel jour aujourd'hui? say kel zhoor o·zhoor·dwee
It's (18 October).	C'est le (dix-huit octobre). say ler (dee·zwee tok·to·brer)
yesterday morning	hier matin ee·yair ma·tun
tomorrow morning	demain matin der·mun ma·tun
yesterday afternoon	hier après-midi ee·yair a·pray·mee·dee
tomorrow afternoon	demain après-midi der·mun a·pray·mee·dee
yesterday evening	hier soir ee·yair swar
tomorrow evening	demain soir der·mun swar
last week	la semaine dernière la ser·men dair·nyair
next week	la semaine prochaine la ser·men pro·shen
last month	le mois dernier ler mwa dair·nyay
next month	le mois prochain ler mwa pro·shen
last year	l'année dernière la·nay dair·nyair
next year	l'année prochaine la·nay pro·shen

Weather

What's the weather like?	Quel temps fait-il? kel tom fay·teel
What's the weather forecast?	Quelles sont les prévisions météo? kel son lay pray·vee·zyon may·tay·yo
It's (very) cold.	Il fait (très) froid. eel fay (tray) frwa
It's hot.	Il fait chaud. eel fay sho
It's raining.	Il pleut. eel pler
It's snowing.	Il neige. eel nezh
It's sunny.	Il fait beau. eel fay bo
It's windy.	Il fait du vent. eel fay dew von

Directions

Where's (a bank)?	Où est-ce qu'il ya (une banque)? oo es·keel ya (ewn bongk)
What's the address?	Quelle est l'adresse? kel ay la·dres
Could you please write it down?	Pourriez-vous l'écrire, s'il vous plaît? poo·ree·yay voo lay·kreer seel voo play

Fast Talk **Negatives**

To make a negative statement, French uses two words – *ne* ner and *pas* pa, both meaning 'not' – around the verb: *je ne sais pas* zher ner say pa (lit: I not know not). With another negative word in the sentence, *pas* is omitted: *je n'ai rien à déclarer* zher nay ryun a day·kla·ray (lit: I not-have nothing to declare).

Can you show me (on the map)?	Pouvez-vous m'indiquer (sur la carte)? poo·vay·voo mun·dee·kay (sewr la kart)
How far is it?	C'est loin? say lwun
Turn at the corner.	Tournez au coin. toor·nay o kwun
Turn at the traffic lights.	Tournez aux feux. toor·nay o fer
Turn left.	Tournez à gauche. toor·nay a gosh
Turn right.	Tournez à droite. toor·nay a drwat
behind ...	derrière ... dair·yair ...
in front of ...	devant ... der·von ...
next to ...	à côté de ... a ko·tay der ...
opposite ...	en face de ... on fas der ...
straight ahead	tout droit too drwa

23

Airport & Transport

≡ Fast Phrases

When's the next (bus)?	Le prochain (bus) passe à quelle heure? ler pro·shun (bews) pas a kel er
Does this (train) stop at ...?	Est-ce que ce (train) s'arrête à ...? es·ker se (trun) sa·ret a ...
One ticket to ..., please.	Un billet pour ..., s'il vous plaît. um bee·yay poor ... seel voo play

At the Airport

I'm here on business.	Je suis ici pour le travail. zher swee zee·see poor ler tra·vai
I'm here on holiday.	Je suis ici pour les vacances. zher swee zee·see poor lay va·kons
I'm here for (three) days.	Je suis ici pour (trois) jours. zher swee zee·see poor (trwa) zhoor

24

I'm here for (two) weeks.	Je suis ici pour (deux) semaines.
	zher swee zee·see poor (der) ser·men
I'm in transit.	Je suis ici de passage.
	zher swee zee·see der pa·sazh
I'm going to (Paris).	Je vais à (Paris).
	zher vay a (pa·ree)
I have nothing to declare.	Je n'ai rien à déclarer.
	zher nay ryun a day·kla·ray
I have something to declare.	J'ai quelque chose à déclarer.
	zhay kel·ker·shoz a day·kla·ray

Getting Around

PHRASE BUILDER

At what time does the ... leave?	À quelle heure part ...?	a kel er par ...
boat	le bateau	ler ba·to
bus	le bus	ler bews
plane	l'avion	la·vyon
train	le train	ler trun

When's the first bus?	Le premier bus passe à quelle heure?
	ler prer·myay bews pas a kel er
When's the last bus?	Le dernier bus passe à quelle heure?
	ler dair·nyay bews pas a kel er
When's the next bus?	Le prochain bus passe à quelle heure?
	ler pro·shun bews pas a kel er

How long does the trip take?	Le trajet dure combien de temps? ler tra·zhay dewr kom·byun der tom
Is it a direct route?	Est-ce que c-est direct? es·ker say dee·rekt
That's my seat.	C'est ma place. say ma plas
Is this seat taken?	Est-ce que cette place est occupée? es·ker set plas ay to·kew·pay
✂ Is it taken?	C'est occupée? say to·kew·pay

Buying Tickets

| Where can I buy a ticket? | Où peut-on acheter un billet?
oo per·ton ash·tay um bee·yay |
| Do I need to book? | Est-ce qu'il faut réserver une place?
es·keel fo ray·zer·vay ewn plas |

Fast Talk — Reading French

In written French, an *l'* in front of a word beginning with a vowel or a silent *h* replaces a *le* or a *la* (the) and is pronounced as if the word starts with an *l*, eg *l'orange* lo·ronzh (orange). Also, if one word ends with a consonant and the next word starts with a vowel or an *h*, run the sounds together as if they were one word – eg *vous avez* voo za·vay (you have). Otherwise don't pronounce a consonant at the end of a word, eg *faux* fo (false) – the exception is final *c*, eg *sec* sek (dry).

| What time do I have to check in? | Il faut se présenter à l'enregistrement à quelle heure? |
| | eel fo ser pray·zon·tay a lon·rer·zhee·strer·mon a kel er |

PHRASE BUILDER

One ... ticket (to Paris), please.	Un billet ... (pour Paris), s'il vous plaît.	um bee·yay ... (poor pa·ree) seel voo play
1st-class	de première classe	der prem·yair klas
2nd-class	de seconde classe	der se·gond klas
child's	au tarif enfant	o ta·reef on·fon
one-way	simple	sum·pler
return	aller et retour	a·lay ay rer·toor
student's	au tarif étudiant	o ta·reef ay·tew·dyon

| I'd like an aisle seat. | Je voudrais une place côté couloir. |
| | zher voo·dray ewn plas ko·tay koo·lwar |

| I'd like a window seat. | Je voudrais une place côté fenêtre. |
| | zher voo·dray ewn plas ko·tay fe·ne·trer |

| I'd like a (non)smoking seat. | Je voudrais une place (non-)fumeur. |
| | zher voo·dray ewn plas (non·)few·mer |

AIRPORT & TRANSPORT

27

Luggage

My luggage has been damaged.	Mes bagages ont été endommagés. may ba·gazh on tay·tay on·do·ma·zhay
My luggage has been stolen.	Mes bagages ont été volés. may ba·gazh on tay·tay vo·lay
My luggage has been lost.	Mes bagages ont été perdus. may ba·gazh on tay·tay per·dew
I'd like a luggage locker.	Je voudrais une consigne automatique. zher voo·dray ewn kon·see·nyer o·to·ma·teek
Can I have some coins/tokens?	Je peux avoir des pièces/jetons? zher per a·vwar day pyes/zher·ton

Bus & Train

Where's the bus stop?	Où est l'arrêt d'autobus? oo ay la·ray do·to·bews
Which bus goes to ...?	Quel bus va à ...? kel bews va a ...
Is this the bus to ...?	Est-ce que c'est le bus pour ...? es·ker say ler bews poor ...
What station is this?	C'est quelle gare? say kel gar
What's the next station?	Quelle est la prochaine gare? kel ay la pro·shen gar

Does this train stop at ...?	Est-ce que ce train s'arrête à ...? es·ker se trun sa·ret a ...
Do I need to change trains?	Est-ce qu'il faut changer de train? es·keel fo shon·zhay der trun
How many stops to ...?	Combien d'arrêts jusqu'à ...? kom·byun da·ray zhews·ka ...
Can you tell me when we get to ...?	Pouvez-vous me dire quand nous arrivons à ...? poo·vay·voo mer deer kon noo za·ree·von a ...
I want to get off at ...	Je veux descendre à ... zher ver day·son·drer a ...
I want to get off here.	Je veux descendre ici. zher ver day·son·drer ee·see

Taxi

Where's the taxi stand?	Où est la station de taxis? oo ay la sta·syon der tak·see
I'd like a taxi at (nine o'clock).	Je voudrais un taxi à (neuf heures). zher voo·dray un tak·see a (ner ver)
Is your taxi free?	Vous êtes libre? voo·zet lee·brer
How much is it to ...?	C'est combien pour aller à ...? say kom·byun poor a·lay a ...
Please put the meter on.	Mettez le compteur, s'il vous plaît. me·tay ler kon·ter seel voo play

Please take me to (this address).	Conduisez-moi à (cette adresse), s'il vous plaît. kon·dwee·zay mwa a (set a·dres) seel voo play
To ...	À ... a ...
Please slow down.	Roulez plus lentement, s'il vous plaît. roo·lay plew lont·mon seel voo play
Please wait here.	Attendez ici, s'il vous plaît. a·ton·day ee·see seel voo play
Stop at the corner.	Arrêtez-vous au coin de la rue. a·ray·tay voo o kwun der la rew
Stop here.	Arrêtez-vous ici. a·ray·tay voo ee·see

Car & Motorbike

I'd like to hire a car.	Je voudrais louer une voiture. zher voo·dray loo·way ewn vwa·tewr
I'd like to hire a motorbike.	Je voudrais louer une moto. zher voo·dray loo·way ewn mo·to
How much for daily hire?	Quel est le tarif par jour? kel ay ler ta·reef par zhoor
How much for weekly hire?	Quel est le tarif par semaine? kel ay ler ta·reef par ser·men
Is this the road to ...?	C'est la route pour ...? say la root poor ...

30

Fast Talk Asking Questions

The easiest way to ask a 'yes/no' question in French is to make a statement with a rise in intonation. Alternatively, you can use *est-ce que* es·ker (lit: is-it that) in front of a statement.

The question words for more specific questions go at the start of the sentence: *comment* ko·mon (how), *qu'est-ce que* kes·ker (what), *quand* kon (when), *où* oo (where), *qui* kee (who) or *pourquoi* poor·kwa (why).

(How long) Can I park here?	(Combien de temps) Est-ce que je peux stationner ici? (kom·byun der tom) es·ker zher per sta·syo·nay ee·see
Where's a petrol station?	Où est-ce qu'il y a une station-service? oo es·keel ya ewn sta·syon·ser·vees

Cycling

Where can I hire a bicycle?	Où est-ce que je peux louer un vélo? oo es·ker zher per loo·way un vay·lo
Are there cycling paths?	Est-ce qu'il y a des pistes cyclables? es·keel ya day peest see·kla·bler
Is there bicycle parking?	Y a-t-il une zone de stationnement pour bicyclettes? ya·teel ewn zon der sta·syon·mon poor bee·see·klet

31

Accommodation

⇛ Fast Phrases

I have a reservation.	J'ai une réservation. zhay ewn ray·zair·va·syon
When/Where is breakfast served?	Quand/Où le petit déjeuner est-il servi? kon/oo ler per·tee day·zher·nay ay·teel sair·vee
What time is checkout?	Quand faut-il régler? kon fo·teel ray·glay

Finding Accommodation

PHRASE BUILDER

Where's a ...?	Où est-ce qu'on peut trouver ...?	oo es·kon per troo·vay ...
bed and breakfast	une pension	ewn pon·syon
camping ground	un terrain de camping	un tay·run der kom·peeng
guesthouse	une pension	ewn pon·see·on
hotel	un hôtel	un o·tel
youth hostel	une auberge de jeunesse	ewn o·bairzh der zher·nes

Booking & Checking In

I have a reservation.	J'ai une réservation. zhay ewn ray·zair·va·syon
Do you have a single room?	Avez-vous une chambre à un lit? a·vay·voo ewn shom·brer a un lee
Do you have a double room?	Avez-vous une chambre avec un grand lit? a·vay·voo ewn shom·brer a·vek ung gron lee
Do you have a twin room?	Avez-vous une chambre avec des lits jumeaux? a·vay·voo ewn shom·brer a·vek day lee zhew·mo
Are there rooms?	Y a-t-il des chambres? ya·teel day shom·brer
How much is it per night?	Quel est le prix par nuit? kel ay ler pree par nwee
How much is it per person?	Quel est le prix par personne? kel ay ler pree par per·son
How much is it per week?	Quel est le prix par semaine? kel ay ler pree par ser·men
For (two) nights.	Pour (deux) nuits. poor (der) nwee
From (July 2) to (July 6).	Du (deux juillet) au (six juillet). dew (der zhwee·yay) o (see zhwee·yay)
Can I see it?	Est-ce que je peux la voir? es·ker zher per la vwar
Is breakfast included?	Le petit déjeuner est-il inclus? ler per·tee day·zher·nay ay·teel un·klew

33

Fast Talk

Using Patterns

Look out for patterns of words or phrases that stay the same, even when the situation changes, eg 'Do you have ...?' or 'I'd like to ...' (see p8). If you can recognise these patterns, you're already halfway to creating a full phrase. The dictionary will help you put other words together with these patterns to convey your meaning – even if it's not completely grammatically correct in all contexts, the dictionary form will always be understood.

| It's fine, I'll take it. | C'est bien, je la prends. say byun zher la pron |
| Do I need to pay upfront? | Est-ce qu'il faut payer par avance? es·keel fo pay·yay par a·vons |

Requests & Questions

When/Where is breakfast served?	Quand/Où le petit déjeuner est-il servi? kon/oo ler per·tee day·zher·nay ay·teel sair·vee
Please wake me at (seven).	Réveillez-moi à (sept) heures, s'il vous plaît. ray·vay·yay·mwa a (set) er seel voo play
Can I have my key, please?	Puis-je avoir ma clé, s'il vous plaît? pweezh av·war ma klay seel voo play
Can I use the kitchen?	Est-ce que je peux utiliser la cuisine? es·ker zher per ew·tee·lee·zay la kwee·zeen

Can I use the telephone?	Est-ce que je peux utiliser le téléphone? es·ker zher per ew·tee·lee·zay ler tay·lay·fon
Can I use the internet?	Est-ce que je peux utiliser l'Internet? es·ker zher per ew·tee·lee·zay lun·tair·net
Do you have an elevator?	Avez-vous un ascenseur? a·vay·voo un a·son·ser
Do you have a laundry service?	Avez-vous un service de blanchisserie? a·vay·voo un sair·vees der blon·shees·ree

Local Knowledge Hotels

Can you recommend somewhere cheap?	Est-ce que vous pouvez recommander un logement pas cher? es·ker voo poo·vay rer·ko·mon·day un lozh·mon pa shair
Can you recommend somewhere nearby?	Est-ce que vous pouvez recommander un logement près d'ici? es·ker voo poo·vay rer·ko·mon·day un lozh·mon pray dee·see
Can you recommend somewhere romantic?	Est-ce que vous pouvez recommander un logement romantique? es·ker voo poo·vay rer·ko·mon·day un lozh·mon ro·mon·teek

Do you have a safe?	Avez-vous un coffre-fort? a·vay·voo ung ko·frer·for
Do you change money here?	Echangez-vous l'argent ici? ay·shon·zhay·voo lar·zhon ee·see
Do you arrange tours here?	Organisez-vous des excursions ici? or·ga·nee·zay·voo day zeks·kewr·syon ee·see

Complaints

| **There's no hot water.** | Il n'y a pas d'eau chaude.
eel nya pa do showd |

PHRASE BUILDER

The ... doesn't work.	... ne fonctionne pas.	... ner fong·syon pa
air-conditioning	La climatisation	la klee·ma·tee·za·syon
heater	L'appareil de chauffage	la·pa·ray der sho·fazh
toilet	Les toilettes	lay twa·let
window	La fenêtre	la fer·ne·trer

It's too dark.	C'est trop sombre. say tro som·brer
It's too noisy.	C'est trop bruyant. say tro brew·yon
It's too small.	C'est trop petit. say tro per·tee

PHRASE BUILDER

Can I get another ...?	Est-ce que je peux avoir un/une autre ...? m/f	es·ker zher per a·vwar un/ewn o·trer ...
blanket	couverture f	koo·vair·tewr
pillow	oreiller m	o·ray·yay
sheet	drap m	drap
towel	serviette f	sair·vee·et

Checking Out

What time is checkout?	Quand faut-il régler? kon fo·teel ray·glay
Can I leave my luggage here until (tonight)?	Puis-je laisser mes bagages jusqu'à (ce soir)? pweezh lay·say may ba·gazh zhews·ka (ser swar)
Can I have my deposit, please?	Est-ce que je pourrais avoir ma caution, s'il vous plaît? es·ker zher poo·ray a·vwar ma ko·syon seel voo play
Can I have my valuables, please?	Est-ce que je pourrais avoir mes biens précieux, s'il vous plaît? es·ker zher poo·ray a·vwar may byun pray·syer seel voo play
I had a great stay, thank you.	J'ai fait un séjour magnifique, merci. zhay fay un say·zhoor ma·nyee·feek mair·see

Eating & Drinking

≡ Fast Phrases

Can I see the menu, please?	Est-ce que je peux voir la carte, s'il vous plaît? es·ker zher per vwar la kart seel voo play
I'd like a (beer), please.	Je voudrais une (bière), s'il vous plaît. zher voo·dray ewn (byair) seel voo play
Please bring the bill.	Apportez-moi l'addition, s'il vous plaît. a·por·tay·mwa la·dee·syon seel voo play

Meals

breakfast	petit déjeuner m per·tee day·zher·nay
lunch	déjeuner m day·zher·nay
dinner	dîner m dee·nay
eat/drink	manger/boire mon·zhay/bwar

Finding a Place to Eat

Can you recommend a bar?	Est-ce que vous pouvez me conseiller un bar? es·ker voo poo·vay mer kon·say·yay um bar
Can you recommend a cafe?	Est-ce que vous pouvez me conseiller un café? es·ker voo poo·vay mer kon·say·yay ung ka·fay
Can you recommend a restaurant?	Est-ce que vous pouvez me conseiller un restaurant? es·ker voo poo·vay mer kon·say·yay un res·to·ron
I'd like to reserve a table for (eight) o'clock.	Je voudrais réserver une table pour (vingt) heures. zher voo·dray ray·zair·vay ewn ta·bler poor (vungt) er
I'd like to reserve a table for (two) people.	Je voudrais réserver une table pour (deux) personnes. zher voo·dray ray·zair·vay ewn ta·bler poor (der) pair·son
✂ **For two, please.**	Pour deux, s'il vous plaît. poor der seel voo play
I'd like a table in the (non)smoking area, please.	Je voudrais une table dans un endroit pour (non-)fumeurs, s'il vous plaît. zher voo·dray ewn ta·bler don zun on·drwa poor (non·)few·mer seel voo play

EATING & DRINKING

39

Local Knowledge — Restaurants

Where would you go for a cheap meal?	Où est-ce qu'on trouve les restaurants bon marché? oo es kon troov lay res·to·ron bom mar·shay
Where would you go for local specialities?	Où est-ce qu'on trouve les spécialités locales? oo es kon troov lay spay·sya·lee·tay lo·kal
Where would you go for a celebration?	On va où pour faire la fête? on va oo poor fair la fet

Are you still serving food?	On peut toujours passer des commandes? om per too·zhoor pa·say day ko·mond
How long is the wait?	Il faut attendre combien de temps? eel fo a·ton·drer kom·byun der tom

Ordering & Paying

Can I see the menu, please?	Est-ce que je peux voir la carte, s'il vous plaît? es·ker zher per vwar la kart seel voo play
✂ **Menu, please.**	La carte, s'il vous plaît. la kart seel voo play

What do you recommend?	Qu'est-ce que vous conseillez? kes·ker voo kon·say·yay
What's the local speciality?	Quelle est la spécialité locale? kel ay la spay·sya·lee·tay lo·kal
I'd like that one, please.	Je voudrais ça, s'il vous plaît. zher voo·dray sa seel voo play
I'd like the wine list, please.	Je voudrais la carte des vins, s'il vous plaît. zher voo·dray la kart day vun seel voo play
We're just having drinks.	C'est juste pour des boissons. say zhewst poor day bwa·son
✂ Just drinks.	Juste des boissons. zhewst day bwa·son

PHRASE BUILDER

I'd like it ...	J'aime ça ...	zhem sa ...
medium	à point	a pwun
rare	saignant	say·nyon
steamed	à la vapeur	a la va·per
well-done	bien cuit	byun kwee
with (the dressing on the side)	avec (la sauce à côté)	a·vek (la sos a ko·tay)
without ...	sans ...	son ...

41

Please bring (a glass).	Apportez-moi (un verre), s'il vous plaît. a·por·tay·mwa (un vair) seel voo play
I didn't order this.	Ce n'est pas ce que j'ai commandé. ser nay pa ser ker zhay ko·mon·day
This is (too) cold.	C'est (trop) froid. say (tro) frwa
That was delicious!	C'était délicieux! say·tay day·lee·syer
Please bring the bill.	Apportez-moi l'addition, s'il vous plaît. a·por·tay·mwa la·dee·syon seel voo play
✂ **Bill, please.**	L'addition, s'il vous plaît. la·dee·syon seel voo play
There's a mistake in the bill.	Il y a une erreur dans la note. eel ya ewn ay·rer don la not

Special Diets & Allergies

Is there a vegetarian restaurant near here?	Y a-t-il un restaurant végétarien par ici? ya·teel un res·to·ron vay·zhay·ta·ryun par ee·see
Do you have vegetarian food?	Vous faites les repas végétariens? voo fet lay rer·pa vay·zhay·ta·ryun

I'm a vegan.	Je suis végétalien(ne). m/f zher swee vay·zhay·ta·lyun/ vay·zhay·ta·lyen
I'm a vegetarian.	Je suis végétarien(ne). m/f zher swee vay·zhay·ta·ryun/ vay·zhay·ta·ryen
I don't eat (red meat).	Je ne mange pas (la viande rouge). zher ner monzh pa (la vyond roozh)
Could you prepare a meal without butter?	Pouvez-vous préparer un repas sans beurre? poo·vay·voo pray·pa·ray un rer·pa son ber
Could you prepare a meal without eggs?	Pouvez-vous préparer un repas sans œufs? poo·vay·voo pray·pa·ray un rer·pa son zer
Could you prepare a meal without meat stock?	Pouvez-vous préparer un repas sans bouillon gras? poo·vay·voo pray·pa·ray un rer·pa son boo·yon gra

Fast Talk   Practising French

If you want to practise your language skills,
try the waiters at a restaurant. Find your feet with straight-
forward phrases such as asking for a table and ordering
a drink, then initiate a conversation by asking for menu
recommendations or asking how a dish is cooked. And as
you'll often know food terms even before you've 'officially'
learnt a word of the language, you're already halfway to
understanding the response.

PHRASE BUILDER

I'm allergic to ...	Je suis allergique ...	zher swee za·lair·zheek ...
dairy produce	aux produits laitiers	o pro·dwee lay·tyay
fish	au poisson	o pwa·son
gluten	au gluten	o glew·ten
MSG	au glutamate de sodium	o glew·ta·mat der so·dyom
pork	au porc	o por
poultry	à la volaille	a la vo·lai
seafood	aux fruits de mer	o frwee der mair
shellfish	aux crustacés	o krew·sta·say

Nonalcoholic Drinks

coffee (without sugar)	café (sans sucre) ka·fay (son sew·krer)
orange juice	jus d'orange zhew do·ronzh
soft drink	boisson non-alcoolisée bwa·son non·al·ko·lee·zay
tea (with milk)	thé (au lait) tay (o lay)
(mineral) water	eau (minérale) o (mee·nay·ral)

Alcoholic Drinks

a shot of (gin)	un petit verre de (gin) um per·tee vair der (zheen)

a bottle of beer	une bouteille de bière
	ewn boo·tay der byair
a glass of beer	un verre de bière
	un vair der byair
a pint of beer	un demi de bière
	un der·mee der byair
a bottle of ... wine	une bouteille de vin ...
	ewn boo·tay der vun ...

PHRASE BUILDER

a glass of ... wine	un verre de vin ...	un vair der vun ...
dessert	de dessert	der day·sair
red	rouge	roozh
rose	rosé	ro·zay
sparkling	mousseux	moo·ser
white	blanc	blong

In the Bar

I'll buy you a drink.	Je vous offre un verre.
	zher voo zo·frer un vair
What would you like?	Qu'est-ce que vous voulez?
	kes·ker voo voo·lay
I'll have ...	Je prends ...
	zher pron ...
Same again, please.	La même chose, s'il vous plaît.
	la mem shoz seel voo play
It's my round.	C'est ma tournée.
	say ma toor·nay
Cheers!	Santé!
	son·tay

Buying Food

How much is (a kilo of cheese)?	C'est combien (le kilo de fromage)? say kom·byun (ler kee·lo der fro·mazh)
Do you have other kinds?	Est-ce que vous avez autre chose? pol es ker voo za·vay o·trer shoz
What's that?	Qu'est-ce que c'est, ça? kes·ker say sa
Can I taste it?	Je peux goûter? zher per goo·tay

PHRASE BUILDER

I'd like ...	Je voudrais ...	zher voo·dray ...
(200) grams	(deux cents) grammes	(der son) gram
(two) kilos	(deux) kilos	(der) kee·lo
(three) pieces	(trois) morceaux	(trwa) mor·so
(six) slices	(six) tranches	(sees) tronsh
some of that/ those	de ça	der sa

Less.	Moins. mwun
Enough.	Ça ira. sa ee·ra
A bit more.	Encore un peu. ong·kor un per

Menu Decoder

This miniguide to French cuisine is designed to help you navigate menus. French nouns, and adjectives affected by gender, have their gender indicated by ⓜ or ①. If it's a plural noun, you'll also see pl.

- a -

à la vapeur a la va·per steamed
abricot ⓜ ab·ree·ko apricot
agneau ⓜ a·nyo lamb
agneau de lait ⓜ a·nyo der lay baby lamb
ail ⓜ ai garlic
aloyau ⓜ a·lwa·yo sirloin
amandes ① pl a·mond almonds
amuse-gueule ⓜ a·mewz·gerl appetizer
ananas ⓜ a·na·nas pineapple
anchois ⓜ on·shwa anchovies
andouille ⓜ on·doo·yer sausage made of intestines
aneth ⓜ a·net dill
anguille ① ong·gee·yer eel
apéritif ⓜ a·pay·ree·teef aperitif
artichaut ⓜ ar·tee·sho artichoke
asperges ① a·spairzh asparagus
au poivre o pwa·vrer with pepper sauce
aubergine ① o·bair·zheen eggplant
avec a·vek with
avocat ⓜ a·vo·ka avocado

- b -

banane ① ba·nan banana
bar ⓜ bar bass

beignet ⓜ be·nyay fritter
betterave ① be·trav beetroot
bière ① byair beer
bifteck ⓜ beef·tek beefsteak
bisque ① beesk shellfish soup
bœuf ⓜ berf beef
bœuf bourguignon ⓜ berf boor·geen·yon beef stew with onions & mushrooms in a burgundy sauce
bouillabaisse ① bwee·ya·bes fish soup from Marseilles
bouilli(e) ⓜ/① boo·yee boiled
bouillon ⓜ boo·yon broth
bourride ① boo·reed Provençal white fish soup
braisé(e) ⓜ/① bre·se braised
brème ① brem bream
brochet ⓜ bro·shay pike

- c -

cacahuètes ① pl ka·ka·wet peanuts
caille ① kay·yer quail
calmar ⓜ kal·mar squid
canard ⓜ ka·nar duck
canard sauvage ⓜ ka·nar so·vazh wild duck
caneton ⓜ kan·ton duckling
carbonnade ① kar·bo·nad selection of chargrilled meats

carottes ① pl ka·rot carrots
carrelet ⓜ ka·re·lay plaice
cassis ⓜ ka·sees blackcurrant
céleri ① sayl·ree celery
cerfeuil ⓜ ser·fer·yee chervil
cerises ① pl ser·rees cherries
cervelle ① sair·vel brains
champignons ⓜ pl shom·pee·nyon mushrooms
châtaignes ① pl sha·tayn·yer chestnuts
chevreuil ⓜ sher·vrer·yer venison
chou ⓜ shoo cabbage
chou-fleur ⓜ shoo·fler cauliflower
choucroute ① shoo·kroot pickled cabbage • sauerkraut
ciboulette ① see·boo·let chives
citron ⓜ see·tron lemon
citrouille ① see·troo·yer pumpkin
cochon de lait ⓜ ko·shon der lay suckling pig
concombre ⓜ kong·kom·brer cucumber
consommé ⓜ kon·so·may clear soup
contre-filet ⓜ kon·trer·fee·lay beef sirloin (steak)
coq au vin ⓜ kok o vun chicken cooked with wine, onions & mushrooms
coquilles Saint-Jacques ① pl ko·kee·yer sun·zhak scallops
cornichon ⓜ kor·nee·shon gherkin
côtelette ① kot·let cutlet
coulis ⓜ koo·lee fruit or vegetable purée
courgette ① koor·zhet zucchini
crevettes grises ① pl krer·vet grees shrimps
crevettes roses ① pl krer·vet ros prawns
cru(e) ⓜ/① krew raw

crudités ⓜ pl krew·dee·tay raw vegetables with dressings
cuisses de grenouilles ① pl kwees de grer·noo·yer frogs' legs
cuit(e) ⓜ/① kwee(t) cooked
cuit(e) au four ⓜ/① kwee(t) o foor baked

- d -

darne ⓜ darn fish cutlet
datte ① dat date
daurade ① do·rad sea bream
dessert ⓜ day·sair dessert
dinde/dindon ①/ⓜ dund/dun·don turkey
dindonneau ⓜ dun·do·no young turkey
doux/douce ⓜ/① doo(s) mild • sweet
du jour dew zhoor of the day

- e -

écrevisses ① pl ay·krer·vees crayfish
émincé(e) ⓜ/① ay·mun·say thinly sliced
entré ① on·tray entree
entrecôte ① on·trer·kot ribsteak
épaule ① ay·pol shoulder
épinards ⓜ pl ay·pee·nar spinach
escargots ⓜ pl es·kar·go snails
estouffade ① es·too·fad stew
estragon ⓜ es·tra·gon tarragon

- f -

faisan ⓜ fer·zon pheasant
fait(e) à la maison ⓜ/① fe(t) a la may·zon homemade
farci(e) ⓜ/① far·see stuffed
fenouil ⓜ fer·noo·yer fennel
figue ① feeg fig

48

filet ⓜ fee·lay fillet
flamiche ⓕ fla·meesh leek quiche
foie ⓜ fwa liver
fraises ⓕ pl frez strawberries
framboises ⓕ pl from·bwaz raspberries
fromage ⓜ fro·mazh cheese
fricassée ⓕ free·ka·say stewed meat & vegetables in creamy sauce
fumé(e) ⓜ/ⓕ few·may smoked

- g -

gambas ⓕ pl gom·bas king prawns
garniture ⓕ gar·nee·tewr garnish
gelée ⓕ zher·lay jelly
gibier ⓜ zheeb·yay game
gigot ⓜ zhee·go leg
grillade ⓕ gree·yad mixed grill
grillé(e) ⓜ/ⓕ gree·yay grilled
groseilles ⓕ pl gro·zay·yer gooseberries

- h -

hachis ⓜ a·shee hash (chopped mince meat or vegetables)
haricots verts ⓜ pl a·ree·ko vair French or string beans
homard ⓜ o·mar Atlantic lobster
huîtres ⓕ pl wee·trer oysters

- j -

jambon ⓜ zhom·bon ham

- l -

laitance ⓕ lay·tons roe
laitue ⓕ lay·tew lettuce
langoustines ⓕ pl long·goo·steen scampi or Dublin Bay prawns
langue ⓕ long tongue

lapin ⓜ la·pun rabbit
lard ⓜ lar bacon
laurier ⓜ lo·ryay bay leaf
légumes ⓜ pl lay·gewm vegetables
lentilles ⓕ pl lon·tee·yer lentils
lièvre ⓜ lye·vrer hare
longe ⓕ lonzh loin
lotte ⓕ lot monkfish
loup de mer ⓜ loo de mer bass

- m -

maison ⓕ may·zon of the house
mange-tout ⓜ monzh·too sugar peas • snowpeas
maquereau ⓜ ma·kro mackerel
mariné(e) ⓜ/ⓕ ma·ree·nay marinated
marjolaine ⓕ mar·zho·len marjoram
marrons ⓜ pl ma·ron chestnuts
menthe ⓕ mont mint
menu dégustation ⓜ mer·new day·gew·sta·syon tasting menu
merguez ⓕ mair·gez spicy red sausage
merlan ⓜ mer·lon whiting
mirabelle ⓕ mee·ra·bel plum
moelle ⓕ mwal bone marrow
moules ⓕ pl mool mussels
moules marinières ⓕ pl mool ma·ree·nyair mussels with shallots in white-wine sauce
moutarde ⓕ moo·tard mustard
mûres ⓕ pl mewr blackberries

- n -

noisettes ⓕ pl nwa·zet hazelnuts
noix ⓕ nwa nuts • walnuts
noix de coco ⓕ nwa der ko·ko coconut

- o -

oie ① wa goose
oignon ⓜ on·yon onion
olives ① pl o·leev olives
orange ① o·ronzh orange

- p -

palourdes ① pl pa·loord clams
pamplemousse ⓜ pom·pler·moos grapefruit
pané(e) ⓜ/① pa·nay crumbed
pastèque ① pas·tek watermelon
patate douce ① pa·tat doos sweet potato
pâté ⓜ pa·tay paté • pie
pâtes ① pl pat pasta
pêche ① pesh peach
persil ⓜ pair·seel parsley
petits pois ⓜ pl per·tee pwa peas
piquant ⓜ pee·kon spicy hot
pistou ⓜ pee·stoo pesto
plat ⓜ **principal** pla prun·see·pal main course
poché(e) ⓜ/① po·shay poached
poêlé(e) ⓜ/① pwa·lay pan-fried
poire ① pwar pear
poireau ⓜ pwa·ro leek
pois chiches ⓜ pl pwa sheesh chickpeas
poisson ⓜ pwa·son fish
poitrine de porc ① pwa·treen de por pork belly
poitrine de veau ① pwa·treen de vo breast of veal
poivre ⓜ pwa·vrer pepper
poivron ⓜ pwa·vron capsicum • pepper
pomme ① pom apple
pomme de terre ① pom der tair potato
porc ⓜ por pork
potage ⓜ po·tazh thick soup, usually vegetable

potiron ⓜ po·tee·ron pumpkin
poularde ① poo·lard fattened chicken
poulet ⓜ poo·lay chicken
poulpe ① poolp octopus
prune ① prewn plum
pruneau ⓜ prew·no prune

- q -

queue de bœuf ① ker de berf oxtail

- r -

radis ⓜ ra·dee radish
ragoût ⓜ ra·goo stew of meat or poultry & vegetables
raifort ⓜ ray·for horseradish
raisins ⓜ pl ray·zun grapes
ratatouille ① ra·ta·too·yer zucchini, eggplant, tomato & garlic dish
rillettes ① pl ree·yet potted meat (pork or goose)
riz ⓜ ree rice
rognons ⓜ pl ron·yon kidneys
romarin ⓜ ro·ma·run rosemary
rôti(e) ⓜ/① ro·tee roast

- s -

saint-pierre ⓜ sun·pyair John Dory (fish)
salade ① sa·lad salad
sanglier ⓜ song·glee·yay wild boar
sardines ① pl sar·deen sardines
sauge ① sozh sage
saumon ⓜ so·mon salmon
séché(e) ⓜ/① say·shay dried
sel ⓜ sel salt
selle ① sel saddle (of meat)
soupe ① soop soup
spiritueux ⓜ pl spee·ree·twer spirits

steak frites ⓜ stek freet steak with chips
steak tartare ⓜ stek tar·tar raw minced beef, raw onion & egg yolk

- t -

thon ⓜ ton tuna
thym ⓜ tun thyme
topinambours ⓜ pl to·pee·nom·boor Jerusalem artichokes
tournedos ⓜ toor·ner·do thick slices of fillet
tourte ⓕ toort pie
tranché(e) ⓜ/ⓕ tron·shay sliced
tripes ⓕ pl treep tripe

truffes ⓕ pl trewf truffles
truite ⓕ trweet trout

- v -

veau ⓜ vo veal
venaison ⓕ ver·nay·zon venison
vinaigre ⓜ vee·nay·grer vinegar
viande ⓕ vyond meat
vin blanc ⓜ vum blong white wine
vin de dessert ⓜ vun der day·sair dessert wine
vin mousseux ⓜ vum moo·ser sparkling wine
vin rouge ⓜ vun roozh red wine
volaille ⓕ vo·lai poultry

Sightseeing

≡ Fast Phrases

When's the museum open?	Le musée ouvre à quelle heure? ler mew·zay oo·vrer a kel er
When's the next tour?	C'est quand la prochaine excursion? say kon la pro·shen eks·kewr·syon
Can I take photographs?	Je peux prendre des photos? zher per pron·drer day fo·to

Planning

Do you have information on local sights?	Avez-vous des renseignements sur les sites locaux à visiter? a·vay·voo day ron·sen·yer·mon sewr lay seet lo·ko a vee·zee·tay
I have (one day).	J'ai (un jour). zhay (un zhoor)

I'd like to see ...	J'aimerais voir ... zhem·ray vwar ...
I'd like to hire a local guide.	Je voudrais faire appel aux services d'un guide. zher voo·dray fair a·pel o sair·vees dung geed
✂ Are there guides?	Y a-t-il des guides? ya·teel day geed

Questions

What's that?	Qu'est-ce que c'est? kes·ker say
How old is it?	Ça date de quand? sa dat der kon
Who made it?	Qui l'a fait? kee la fay
Can I take photographs?	Je peux prendre des photos? zher per pron·drer day fo·to
Could you take a photo of me?	Pouvez-vous me prendre en photo? poo·vay·voo mer pron·drer un fo·to

PHRASE BUILDER

I'd like a/an ...	Je voudrais ...	zher voo·dray ...
audio set	un écouteur	un ay·koo·ter
catalogue	un catalogue	ung ka·ta·log
guidebook (in English)	un guide (en anglais)	ung geed (on ong·lay)
local map	une carte de la région	ewn kart der la ray·zhyon

Getting In

What time does it open?	Quelle est l'heure d'ouverture? kel ay ler doo·vair·tewr
What time does it close?	Quelle est l'heure de fermeture? kel ay ler der fer·mer·tewr
What's the admission charge?	Quel est le prix d'admission? kel ay ler pree dad·mee·syon

PHRASE BUILDER

Is there a discount for ...?	Il y a une réduction pour les ...?	eel ya ewn ray·dewk·syon poor lay ...
children	enfants	zon·fon
families	familles	fa·mee·yer
groups	groupes	groop
older people	seniors	say·nyor
students	étudiants	zay·tew·dyon

Galleries & Museums

When's the gallery open?	La galerie ouvre à quelle heure? la gal·ree oo·vrer a kel er
When's the museum open?	Le musée ouvre à quelle heure? ler mew·zay oo·vrer a kel er
What's in the collection?	Qu'est-ce qu'il y a dans la collection? kes·keel·ya don la ko·lek·syon
It's a/an ... exhibition.	C'est une exposition ... set ewn ek·spo·zee·syon ...

I like the works of ...	J'aime l'œuvre de ... zhem ler·vrer der ...

PHRASE BUILDER

... art	l'art ...	lar ...
contemporary	contemporain	kon·tom·po·run
impressionist	impressionniste	um·pray·syo·neest
modernist	moderniste	mo·dair·neest
Renaissance	de la Renaissance	der la rer·nay·sons

Tours

When's the next tour?	C'est quand la prochaine excursion? say kon la pro·shen eks·kewr·syon
Is food included?	Est-ce que la nourriture est incluse? es·ker la noo·ree·tewr ay tung·klewz

55

Local Knowledge — Tours

Can you recommend a tour?	Pouvez-vous me recommander une excursion? poo·vay·voo mer rer·ko·mon·day ewn eks·kewr·syon
Can you recommend a boat trip?	Pouvez-vous me recommander une excursion en bateau? poo·vay·voo mer rer·ko·mon·day ewn eks·kewr·syon om ba·to
Can you recommend a day trip?	Pouvez-vous me recommander une excursion d'une journée? poo·vay·voo mer rer·ko·mon·day ewn eks·kewr·syon dewn zhoor·nay

Is transport included?	Est-ce que le transport est inclus? es·ker ler trons·por ay tung·klew
Do I need to take ...?	Dois-je prendre ...? dwa·zher pron·drer ...
How long is the tour?	L'excursion dure combien de temps? leks·kewr·syon dewr kom·byun der tom
What time should we be back?	On doit rentrer pour quelle heure? on dwa ron·tray poor kel er
I've lost my group.	J'ai perdu mon groupe. zhay pair·dew mon groop

Shopping

≡ Fast Phrases

Can I look at it?	Est-ce que je peux le voir?
	es·ker zher per ler vwar
How much is it?	C'est combien?
	say kom·byun
That's too expensive.	C'est trop cher.
	say tro shair

Looking For ...

Where's (a market)?	Où est-ce qu'il y a (un marché)?
	oo es·keel ya (un mar·shay)
Where can I buy (locally produced goods)?	Où puis-je acheter (des marchandises produits localement)?
	oo pweezh ash·tay (day mar·shon·deez pro·dwee lo·kal·mon)

In the Shop

I'd like to buy ...	Je voudrais acheter ...
	zher voo·dray ash·tay ...

Local Knowledge — Shops

Where would you go for bargains?	Où est-ce qu'on va pour des marchandises bon marché? oo es·kon va poor day mar·shon·deez bom mar·shay
Where would you go for souvenirs?	Où est-ce qu'on va pour des souvenirs locales? oo es·kon va poor day soov·neer lo·kal

I'm just looking.	Je regarde. zher rer·gard
Can I look at it?	Est-ce que je peux le voir? es·ker zher per ler vwar
What is this made from?	C'est fabriqué avec quoi? say fa·bree·kay a·vek kwa
Do you have any others?	Vous en avez d'autres? voo zon a·vay do·trer
Does it have a guarantee?	Est-ce qu'il y a une garantie? es keel ya ewn ga·ron·tee
It's faulty.	C'est défectueux. say day·fek·twer
It's broken.	C'est cassé. say ka·say
Can I have it wrapped?	Pouvez-vous l'envelopper? poo·vay·voo lon·vlo·pay
Can I have it sent overseas?	Pouvez-vous me l'envoyer à l'étranger? poo·vay·voo mer lon·vwa·yay a lay·tron·zhay

Can I have a bag, please?	Puis-je avoir un sac, s'il vous plaît? pweezh a·vwar un sak seel voo play
I'd like my money back, please.	Je voudrais un remboursement, s'il vous plaît. zher voo·dray un rom·boors·mon seel voo play
I'd like to return this, please.	Je voudrais rapporter ceci, s'il vous plaît. zher voo·dray ra·por·tay ser·see seel voo play

Paying & Bargaining

How much is it?	C'est combien? say kom·byun
✂ How much?	Combien? kom·byun
It's (12) euros.	C'est (douze) euros. say (dooz) er·ro
Can you write down the price?	Pouvez-vous écrire le prix? poo·vay·voo ay·kreer ler pree
Can you lower the price?	Vous pouvez baisser le prix? voo poo·vay bay·say ler pree
That's too expensive.	C'est trop cher. say tro shair
Do you have something cheaper?	Avez-vous quelque chose de moins cher? a·vay·voo kel·ker shoz der mwun shair
I'll give you ...	Je vous donnerai ... zher voo don·ray ...

Fast Talk **False Friends**

Some French words look like English words but have a different meaning altogether! For example, *car* kar is 'coach/bus' (not 'car', which is *voiture* vwa·tewr); *menu* me·new is 'set menu' (not 'menu', which is *carte* kart); *information* un·for·ma·syon is 'news' (not 'information', which is *renseignement* ron·sen·yer·mon); and *librairie* lee·bray·ree is 'bookshop' (not 'library', which is *bibliothèque* bee·blee·o·tek).

Do you accept credit cards?	Est-ce que je peux payer avec une carte de crédit? es·ker zher per pay·yay a·vek ewn kart der kray·dee
I'd like my change, please.	Je voudrais ma monnaie, s'il vous plaît. zher voo·dray ma mo·nay seel voo play
Can I have a receipt, please?	Puis-je avoir un reçu, s'il vous plaît? pweezh a·vwar un rer·sew seel voo play
✂ Receipt, please.	Un reçu, s'il vous plaît. un rer·sew seel voo play

Clothes & Shoes

| I'm looking for shoes. | Je cherche des chaussures.
zher shairsh day sho·sewr |
| I'm looking for underwear. | Je cherche des sous-vêtements.
zher shairsh day soo·vet·mon |

60

My size is (medium).	Je fais du (moyen).
	zher fay dew (mwa·yen)
Can I try it on?	Puis-je l'essayer?
	pwee·zher lay·say·yay
It doesn't fit.	Ce n'est pas la bonne taille.
	ser nay pa la bon tai
It's too big.	C'est trop grand.
	say tro gron
It's too small.	C'est trop petit.
	say tro per·tee

Books & Reading

Is there an English-language bookshop?	Y a-t-il une librairie de langue anglaise?
	ya·teel ewn lee·brair·ee der long ong·glayz
Is there an English-language section?	Y a-t-il un rayon anglais?
	ya·teel un ray·yon ong·glay
Can you recommend a book for me?	Pouvez-vous me conseiller un roman?
	poo·vay·voo mer kon·say·yay un ro·mon
I'm looking for something by ...	Je cherche quelque chose de ...
	zher shairsh kel·ker shoz der ...
I'd like a dictionary.	Je voudrais un dictionnaire.
	zher voo·dray un deek·syo·nair
I'd like a newspaper (in English).	Je voudrais un journal (en anglais).
	zher voo·dray un zhoor·nal (on ong·glay)

Fast Talk **Money Slang**

You may hear these slang terms for 'money', so be prepared to recognise them: *blé* blay, *flouze* flooz, *pèze* pez or *pognon* po·nyon.

Music & DVDs

I'd like a CD/DVD.	Je voudrais un CD/DVD. zher voo·dray un say·day/ day·vay·day
I'd like some headphones.	Je voudrais un casque. zher voo·dray ung kask
What's his/her best recording?	Quel est son meilleur enregistrement? kel ay som may·yer on·rer·zhees·trer·mon
Can I listen to it here?	Je peux l'écouter ici? zher per lay·koo·tay ee·see
What region is this DVD for?	Pour quelle région ce DVD est-il codé? poor kel ray·zhyon ser day·vay·day ay·teel ko·day

Entertainment

≡ Fast Phrases

What's on tonight?	Qu'est-ce qu'on joue ce soir? kes·kon zhoo ser swar
Where are the clubs?	Où sont les clubs? oo son lay klerb
When will we meet?	On se retrouve à quelle heure? on ser rer·troov a kel er
Where will we meet?	On se retrouve où? on ser rer·troov oo

Going Out

What's there to do in the evenings?	Qu'est-ce qu'on peut faire le soir? kes·kon per fair ler swar
What's on today?	Qu'est-ce qu'on joue aujourd'hui? kes·kon zhoo o·zhoor·dwee
What's on tonight?	Qu'est-ce qu'on joue ce soir? kes·kon zhoo ser swar
✂ **What's on?**	Qu'est-ce qu'on joue? kes·kon zhoo

Conversation Dos & Don'ts

Sport and culture are safe areas of conversation and food is a sure way to get a French person speaking, but money talk (prices, income etc) is best avoided.

What's on this weekend?	Qu'est-ce qu'on joue ce week-end? kes·kon zhoo ser wee·kend
Is there a local entertainment guide?	Y a-t-il un programme des spectacles? ya·teel un pro·gram day spek·ta·kler
Is there a local gay guide?	Y a-t-il un guide des endroits gais? ya·teel un geed day zon·drwa gay

PHRASE BUILDER

I'd like to go to a/the ...	Je voudrais aller ...	zher voo·dray a·lay ...
ballet	au ballet	o ba·lay
bar	au bar	o bar
cafe	au café	o ka·fay
cinema	au cinéma	o see·nay·ma
concert	à un concert	a ung kon·sair
nightclub	en boîte	on bwat
opera	à l'opéra	a lo·pay·ra
pub	au pub	o perb
restaurant	au restaurant	o res·to·ron
theatre	au théâtre	o tay·a·trer

Local Knowledge Clubs

Can you recommend clubs?	Pouvez-vous me recommander des clubs? poo·vay·voo mer rer·ko·mon·day day klerb
Can you recommend gay venues?	Pouvez-vous me recommander des boîtes gaies? poo·vay·voo mer rer·ko·mon·day day bwat gay
Can you recommend pubs?	Pouvez-vous me recommander des pubs? poo·vay·voo mer rer·ko·mon·day day perb

Meeting Up

When shall we meet?	On se retrouve à quelle heure? on ser rer·troov a kel er
Let's meet at (eight o'clock).	On peut se retrouver à (huit heures). on per ser rer·troo·vay a (wee ter)
Where will we meet?	On se retrouve où? on ser rer·troov oo
Let's meet at (the entrance).	On peut se retrouver devant (l'entrée). on per ser rer·troo·vay der·von (lon·tray)
I'll pick you up.	Je viendrai te chercher. zher vyun·dray ter shair·shay
Sorry I'm late.	Désolé d'être en retard. day·zo·lay de·trer on rer·tar

Practicalities

⇒ Fast Phrases

Where's the nearest ATM?	Où est le guichet automatique le plus proche? oo ay ler gee·shay o·to·ma·teek ler plew prosh
Is there wireless internet access here?	Avez-vous le wifi ici? a·vay·voo ler wee·fee ee·see
Where are the toilets?	Où sont les toilettes? oo son lay twa·let

Banking

Where's a bank?	Où est-ce qu'il y a une banque? oo es·keel ya ewn bongk
What time does the bank open?	À quelle heure ouvre la banque? a kel er oo·vrer la bongk
Where's the nearest ATM?	Où est le guichet automatique le plus proche? oo ay ler gee·shay o·to·ma·teek ler plew prosh
Where's the nearest foreign exchange office?	Où est le bureau de change le plus proche? oo ay ler bew·ro der shonzh ler plew prosh

Where can I (change money)?	Où est-ce que je peux (changer de l'argent)? oo es·ker zher per (shon·zhay der lar·zhon)
I'd like to (withdraw money).	Je voudrais (retirer de l'argent). zher voo·dray (rer·tee·ray der lar·zhon)
What's the exchange rate?	Quel est le taux de change? kel ay ler to der shonzh
What's the charge for that?	Quel est le tarif pour cela? kel ay ler ta·reef poor ser·la

Phone/Mobile Phone

Where's the nearest public phone?	Où est le téléphone public le plus proche? oo ay ler tay·lay·fon pewb·leek ler plew prosh
I'd like to buy a phonecard.	Je voudrais acheter une carte téléphonique. zher voo·dray ash·tay ewn kart tay·lay·fo·neek
I want to make a call to (Singapore).	Je veux téléphoner à (Singapour). zher ver tay·lay·fo·nay a (sung·ga·poor)
I want to make a reverse-charge/collect call.	Je veux téléphoner en PCV. zher ver tay·lay·fo·nay om pay·say·vay

How much is a (three)-minute call?	Quel est le prix d'une communication de (trois) minutes? kel ay ler pree dewn ko·mew·nee·ka·syon der (trwa) mee·newt
The number is ...	Le numéro est ... ler new·may·ro ay ...
I've been cut off.	J'ai été coupé(e). m/f zhay ay·tay koo·pay
It's busy.	La ligne est occupée. la lee·nyer ay to·kew·pay
I'd like a charger for my phone.	Je voudrais un chargeur pour mon portable. zher voo·dray un shar·zher poor mom por·ta·bler
I'd like a SIM card for the network.	Je voudrais une carte SIM pour le réseau. zher voo·dray ewn kart seem poor ler ray·zo

Internet

Where's the local internet cafe?	Où est le cybercafé du coin? oo ay ler see·bair·ka·fay dew kwun
Is there wireless internet access here?	Avez-vous le wifi ici? a·vay·voo ler wee·fee ee·see
Can I connect my laptop here?	Est-ce que je peux utiliser mon ordinateur portable ici? es·ker zher per ew·tee·lee·zay mong or·dee·na·ter por·ta·bler ee·see

Do you have headphones (with a microphone)?	Avez-vous un casque (avec un micro)? a·vay·voo ung kask (a·vek ung mee·kro)

PHRASE BUILDER

I'd like to ...	Je voudrais ...	zher voo·dray ...
burn a CD	brûler un CD	brew·lay un se·de
check my email	consulter mon courrier	kon·sewl·tay mong koo·ryay
download my photos	télécharger mes photos	tay·lay·shar·zhay may fo·to
use a printer	utiliser une imprimante	ew·tee·lee·zay ewn um·pree·mont
use a scanner	utiliser un scanner	ew·tee·lee·zay un ska·nair
use Skype	utiliser Skype	ew·tee·lee·zay skaip

How much per hour?	C'est combien l'heure? say kom·byun ler
How much per page?	C'est combien la page? say kom·byun la pazh
How do I log on?	Comment faire pour me connecter? ko·mon fair poor mer ko·nek·tay
It's crashed.	C'est tombé en panne. say tom·bay om pan
I've finished.	J'ai terminé. zhay tair·mee·nay

Can I connect (my camera) to this computer?	Est-ce que je peux brancher (mon appareil photo) sur cet ordinateur? es·ker zher per bron·shay (mong na·pa·ray fo·to) sewr set or·dee·na·ter

Emergencies

Help!	Au secours! o skoor
Stop!	Arrêtez! a·ray·tay
Go away!	Allez-vous-en! a·lay·voo·zon
Leave me alone!	Laissez-moi tranquille! lay·say·mwa trong·keel
Thief!	Au voleur! o vo·ler

Fast Talk — Understanding French

Most sentences are composed of several words (or parts of words) serving various grammatical functions, as well as those that carry meaning (primarily nouns and verbs). If you're finding it hard to understand what someone is saying to you, listen out for the nouns and verbs to work out the context – this shouldn't be hard as they are usually more emphasised in speech. If you're still having trouble, a useful phrase to know is *Pourriez-vous parler plus lentement, s'il vous plaît?* poo·ree·yay voo par·lay plew lon·ter·mon seel voo play (Could you please speak more slowly?).

Fire!	Au feu!	o fer
Watch out!	Faites attention!	fet a·ton·syon
It's an emergency!	C'est urgent!	say tewr·zhon
There's been an accident.	Il y a eu un accident.	eel ya ew un ak·see·don
Call the police!	Appelez la police!	a·play la po·lees
Call a doctor!	Appelez un médecin!	a·play un mayd·sun
Do you have a first-aid kit?	Avez-vous une trousse de première urgence?	a·vay·voo ewn troos der prer·myair ewr·zhons
Can you help me, please?	Est-ce que vous pourriez m'aider, s'il vous plaît?	es·ker voo poo·ryay may·day seel voo play
Please help me!	Aidez-moi, s'il vous plaît!	ay·day·mwa seel voo play
Can I use the telephone?	Est-ce que je pourrais utiliser le téléphone?	es·ker zher poo·ray ew·tee·lee·zay ler tay·lay·fon
Where are the toilets?	Où sont les toilettes?	oo son lay twa·let
I'm lost.	Je suis perdu(e). m/f	zher swee pair·dew

Police

Where's the police station?	Où est le commissariat de police? oo ay ler ko·mee·sar·ya der po·lees
I've been raped.	J'ai été violé(e). m/f zhay ay·tay vyo·lay
I've been robbed.	On m'a volé. on ma vo·lay
I've lost (my bags).	J'ai perdu (mes valises). zhay pair·dew (may va·leez)
I've lost (my passport).	J'ai perdu (mon passeport). zhay pair·dew (mom pas·por)
(My money) was stolen.	On m'a volé (mon argent). on ma vo·lay (mon ar·zhon)
I want to contact my embassy.	Je veux contacter mon ambassade. zher ver kon·tak·tay mon om·ba·sad
I want to contact my consulate.	Je veux contacter mon consulat. zher ver kon·tak·tay mon kon·sew·la
I have insurance.	J'ai une assurance. zhay ewn a·sew·rons

Health

Where's a nearby chemist?	Où y a-t-il une pharmacie par ici? oo ya·teel ewn far·ma·see par ee·see

Where's a nearby dentist?	Où y a-t-il un dentiste par ici? oo ya·teel un don·teest par ee·see
Where's a nearby hospital?	Où y a-t-il un hôpital par ici? oo ya·teel un o·pee·tal par ee·see
I need a doctor (who speaks English).	J'ai besoin d'un médecin (qui parle anglais). zhay ber·zwun dun mayd·sun (kee parl ong·glay)
Could I see a female doctor?	Est-ce que je peux voir une femme médecin? es·ker zher per vwar ewn fam mayd·sun
I'm sick.	Je suis malade. zher swee ma·lad
It hurts here.	J'ai une douleur ici. zhay ewn doo·ler ee·see
I've been vomiting.	J'ai vomi. zhay vo·mee
I feel nauseous.	J'ai des nausées. zhay day no·zay
I feel dizzy.	J'ai des frissons. zhay day free·son

PHRASE BUILDER

I have (a/an) ...	J'ai ...	zhay ...
cold	un rhume	un rewm
diarrhoea	la diarrhée	la dya·ray
fever	de la fièvre	der la fyay·vrer
headache	mal à la tête	mal a la tet
infection	une infection	ewn un·fek·syon
toothache	mal aux dents	mal o don

Fast Talk Addressing People

The French can seem very formal about addressing people they don't know. They use *Monsieur* mer·syer (Mr), *Madame* ma·dam (Ms/Mrs) or *Mademoiselle* mad·mwa·zel (Miss) where English speakers would use no term of address at all.

I'm on medication for ...	Je prends des médicaments pour ... zher pron day may·dee·ka·mon poor ...
I need something for ...	J'ai besoin d'un médicament pour ... zhay ber·zwun dun may·dee·ka·mom poor ...
My prescription is ...	Mon ordonnance indique ... mon or·do·nons on·deek ...
I'm allergic (to antibiotics).	Je suis allergique (aux antibiotiques). zher swee za·lair·zheek (o zon·tee·byo·teek)
I have a skin allergy.	J'ai une allergie de peau. zhay ewn a·lair·zhee der po

Dictionary

ENGLISH *to* FRENCH

anglais – français

Nouns in this dictionary have their gender indicated by ⓜ or ⓕ. If it's a plural noun, you'll also see pl. Where a word that could be either a noun or a verb has no gender indicated, it's a verb.

- *a* -

accommodation logement ⓜ lozh·mon

account compte ⓜ kont

afternoon après-midi ⓜ a·pray·mee·dee

air-conditioned climatisé kee·ma·tee·zay

airplane avion ⓜ a·vyon

airport aéroport ⓜ a·ay·ro·por

alarm clock réveil ⓜ ray·vay

alcohol alcool ⓜ al·kol

appointment rendez-vous ⓜ ron·day·voo

arrivals arrivées ⓕ a·ree·vay

art gallery galerie ⓕ gal·ree

ashtray cendrier ⓜ son·dree·yay

at à a

ATM guichet ⓜ automatique de banque (GAB) gee·shay o·to·ma·teek der bonk

autumn automne ⓜ o·ton

- *b* -

B&W (film) noir et blanc nwar ay blong

baby bébé ⓜ bay·bay

back (body) dos ⓜ do

backpack sac ⓜ à dos sak a do

bad mauvais(e) ⓜ/ⓕ mo·vay(z)

bag sac ⓜ sak

baggage bagages ⓜ ba·gazh

baggage allowance franchise ⓕ fron·sheez

75

baggage claim retrait ⓜ des bagages
rer·tray day ba·gazh
bakery boulangerie ⓕ boo·lon·zhree
Band-Aid sparadrap ⓜ spa·ra·dra
bank banque ⓕ bongk
bank account compte ⓜ bancaire
kont bong·kair
bath baignoire ⓕ be·nywar
bathroom salle ⓕ de bain sal der bun
battery pile ⓕ peel
beach plage ⓕ plazh
beautiful beau/belle ⓜ/ⓕ bo/bel
beauty salon salon ⓜ de beauté
sa·lon der bo·tay
bed lit ⓜ lee
bed linen draps ⓜ dra
bedroom chambre ⓕ à coucher
shom·brer a koo·shay
beer bière ⓕ byair
bicycle vélo ⓜ vay·lo
big grand(e) ⓜ/ⓕ gron(d)
bill (restaurant) addition ⓕ
a·dee·syon
birthday anniversaire ⓜ
a·nee·vair·sair
blanket couverture ⓕ koo·vair·tewr
blood group groupe ⓜ sanguin groop
song·gun
boarding house pension ⓕ pon·syon
boarding pass carte ⓕ
d'embarquement kart
dom·bar·ker·mon
boat bateau ⓜ ba·to
book livre ⓜ leev·rer
book (make a booking) réserver
ray·zair·vay
booked up complet/complète ⓜ/ⓕ
kom·play/kom·plet
bookshop librairie ⓕ lee·bray·ree
border frontière ⓕ fron·tyair
bottle bouteille ⓕ boo·tay
box boîte ⓕ bwat
boy garçon ⓜ gar·son
boyfriend petit ami ⓜ per·tee ta·mee

bra soutien-gorge ⓜ soo·tyung·gorzh
brakes freins ⓜ frun
bread pain ⓜ pun
briefcase serviette ⓕ sair·vyet
broken cassé(e) ⓜ/ⓕ ka·say
brother frère ⓜ frair
brown brun/brune ⓜ/ⓕ brun/brewn
building bâtiment ⓜ ba·tee·mon
bus (city) (auto)bus ⓜ (o·to·)bews
bus (intercity) (auto)car ⓜ
(o·to·)kar
bus station gare ⓕ routière gar
roo·tyair
bus stop arrêt ⓜ d'autobus a·ray
do·to·bews
business affaires ⓕ a·fair
business class classe ⓕ affaires
klas a·fair
busy occupé(e) ⓜ/ⓕ o·kew·pay
butcher's shop boucherie ⓕ
boosh·ree

-C-

cafe café ⓜ ka·fay
call appeler a·play
camera appareil ⓜ photo a·pa·ray
fo·to
can (tin) boîte ⓕ bwat
cancel annuler a·new·lay
car voiture ⓕ vwa·tewr
car hire location ⓕ de voitures
lo·ka·syon der vwa·tewr
car owner's title carte grise ⓕ kart
greez
car registration immatriculation
ee·ma·tree·kew·la·syon
cash argent ⓜ ar·zhon
cashier caissier/caissière ⓜ/ⓕ
kay·syay/kay·syair
chairlift (skiing) télésiège ⓜ
tay·lay·syezh
change changer shon·zhay
change (coins) monnaie ⓕ mo·nay

change (money) échanger
ay·shon·zhay
check (banking) chèque ⓜ shek
check (bill) addition ⓕ a·dee·syon
check-in (desk) enregistrement
on·rer·zhee·strer·mon
cheque (banking) chèque ⓜ shek
child enfant ⓜ&ⓕ on·fon
church église ⓕ ay·gleez
cigarette lighter briquet ⓜ bree·kay
city ville ⓕ veel
city centre centre-ville ⓜ son·trer·veel
clean propre pro·prer
cleaning nettoyage ⓜ net·wa·yazh
cloakroom vestiaire ⓜ vays·tyair
closed fermé(e) ⓜ/ⓕ fair·may
clothing vêtements ⓜ vet·mon
coat manteau ⓜ mon·to
coffee café ⓜ ka·fay
coins pièces ⓕ pyes
cold froid(e) ⓜ/ⓕ frwa(d)
comfortable confortable
kon·for·ta·bler
company entreprise ⓕ on·trer·preez
computer ordinateur ⓜ or·dee·na·ter
condom préservatif ⓜ
pray·zair·va·teef
confirm (a booking) confirmer
kon·feer·may
connection rapport ⓜ ra·por
convenience store supérette ⓕ de
quartier sew·pay·ret der kar·tyay
cook cuire kweer
cool frais/fraîche ⓜ/ⓕ fray/fresh
cough toux ⓕ too
countryside campagne ⓕ
kom·pa·nyer
cover charge couvert ⓜ koo·vair
crafts artisanat ⓜ ar·tee·za·na
credit card carte ⓕ de crédit kart der
kray·dee
currency exchange taux ⓜ de
change to der shonzh
customs douane ⓕ dwan

-d-

daily quotidien(ne) ⓜ/ⓕ
ko·tee·dyun/ko·tee·dyen
date (day) date ⓕ dat
date of birth date ⓕ de naissance
dat der nay·sons
daughter fille ⓕ fee·yer
day jour ⓜ zhoor
day after tomorrow après-demain
a·pray·der·mun
day before yesterday avant-hier
a·von·tyair
delay retard ⓜ rer·tar
delicatessen charcuterie ⓕ
shar·kew·tree
depart (leave) partir par·teer
department store grand magasin ⓜ
gron ma·ga·zun
departure départ ⓜ day·par
deposit dépôt ⓜ day·po
diaper couche ⓕ koosh
dictionary dictionnaire ⓜ
deek·syo·nair
dinner dîner ⓜ dee·nay
direct direct(e) ⓜ/ⓕ dee·rekt
dirty sale sal
discount remise ⓕ rer·meez
dish plat ⓜ pla
doctor médecin ⓜ mayd·sun
dog ⓜ chien shyun
double bed grand lit ⓜ gron lee
double room chambre ⓕ pour
deux personnes shom·brer poor der
pair·son
dress robe ⓕ rob
drink boire bwar
drink (alcoholic) verre ⓜ vair
drink (beverage) boisson ⓕ bwa·son
drivers licence permis ⓜ de conduire
pair·mee der kon·dweer
drunk ivre ee·vrer
dry sec/sèche ⓜ/ⓕ sek/sesh

-e-

each chaque shak
early tôt to
east est ⓜ est
eat manger mon·zhay
economy class classe ⓕ touriste klas too·reest
elevator ascenseur ⓜ a·son·ser
embassy ambassade ⓕ om·ba·sad
English anglais(e) ⓜ/ⓕ ong·glay(z)
enough assez a·say
entry entrée ⓕ on·tray
envelope enveloppe ⓕ on·vlop
evening soir ⓜ swar
every chaque shak
everything tout too
excess (baggage) excédent ek·say·don
exchange échanger ay·shon·zhay
exhibition exposition ⓕ ek·spo·zee·syon
exit sortie ⓕ sor·tee
expensive cher/chère ⓜ/ⓕ shair
express (mail) exprès eks·pres

-f-

fall (autumn) automne ⓜ o·ton
family famille ⓕ fa·mee·yer
fare tarif ⓜ ta·reef
fashion mode ⓕ mod
fast rapide ra·peed
father père ⓜ pair
ferry bac ⓜ bak
fever fièvre ⓕ fyev·rer
film (for camera) pellicule ⓕ pay·lee·kewl
fine (penalty) amende ⓕ a·mond
finger doigt ⓜ dwa
first class première classe ⓕ prer·myair klas
fish shop poissonnerie ⓕ pwa·son·ree

fleamarket marché ⓜ aux puces mar·shay o pews
flight vol ⓜ vol
floor (storey) étage ⓜ ay·tazh
flu grippe ⓕ greep
footpath sentier ⓜ son·tyay
foreign étranger/étrangère ⓜ/ⓕ ay·tron·zhay/ay·tron·zhair
forest forêt ⓕ fo·ray
free (available) disponible dees·po·nee·bler
free (gratis) gratuit(e) ⓜ/ⓕ gra·twee(t)
fresh frais/fraîche ⓜ/ⓕ fray/fresh
friend ami/amie ⓜ/ⓕ a·mee

-g-

garden jardin ⓜ zhar·dun
gas (for cooking) gaz ⓜ gaz
gas (petrol) essence ⓕ e·sons
gift cadeau ⓜ ka·do
girl fille ⓕ fee·yer
girlfriend petite amie ⓕ per·teet a·mee
glasses (spectacles) lunettes ⓕ pl lew·net
gloves gants ⓜ pl gon
go aller a·lay
go out sortir sor·teer
gold or ⓜ or
grateful reconnaissant(e) ⓜ/ⓕ rer·ko·nay·son(t)
grocery épicerie ⓕ ay·pee·sree
guesthouse pension ⓕ (de famille) pon·syon (der fa·mee·yer)
guided tour visite ⓕ guidée vee·zeet gee·day

-h-

half moitié ⓕ mwa·tyay
handsome beau/belle ⓜ/ⓕ bo/bel

heated chauffé(e) ⓜ/ⓕ sho·fay
help aider ay·day
here ici ee·see
highway autoroute ⓕ o·to·root
hire louer loo·ay
holidays vacances ⓕ pl va·kons
honeymoon lune ⓕ de miel lewn
der myel
hospital hôpital ⓜ o·pee·tal
hot chaud(e) ⓜ/ⓕ show(d)
hotel hôtel ⓜ o·tel
hour heure ⓕ er
husband mari ⓜ ma·ree

- i -

identification card (ID) carte ⓕ
d'identité kart dee·don·tee·tay
ill malade ma·lad
included compris(e) ⓜ/ⓕ kom·pree(z)
information renseignements ⓜ pl
ron·sen·yer·mon
insurance assurance ⓕ a·sew·rons
intermission entracte ⓜ on·trakt
internet cafe cybercafé ⓜ
see·bair·ka·fay
interpreter interprète ⓜ/ⓕ
un·tair·pret
itinerary itinéraire ⓜ ee·tee·nay·rair

- j -

jacket veste ⓕ vest
jeans jean ⓜ zheen
jewellery bijoux ⓜ pl bee·zhoo
journey voyage ⓜ vwa·yazh
jumper (sweater) pull ⓜ pewl

- k -

key clé ⓕ klay
kind (nice) gentil(le) ⓜ/ⓕ zhon·tee
kitchen cuisine ⓕ kwee·zeen

- l -

last (previous) dernier/dernière ⓜ/ⓕ
dair·nyay/dair·nyair
late en retard on rer·tar
later plus tard plew·tar
launderette laverie ⓕ lav·ree
laundry (place) blanchisserie ⓕ
blon·shees·ree
laundry (clothes) linge ⓜ lunzh
leather cuir ⓜ kweer
left luggage (office) consigne ⓕ
kon·see·nyer
letter lettre ⓕ lay·trer
lift (elevator) ascenseur ⓜ a·son·ser
linen (material) lin ⓜ lun
linen (sheets etc) linge ⓜ lunzh
locked fermé(e) à clé ⓜ/ⓕ fair·may
a klay
lost perdu(e) ⓜ/ⓕ pair·dew
lost property office bureau ⓜ des
objets trouvés bew·ro day zob·zhay
troo·vay
luggage bagages ⓜ pl ba·gazh
luggage lockers consigne ⓕ
automatique kon·see·nyer o·to·ma·teek
lunch déjeuner ⓜ day·zher·nay

- m -

mail (postal system) poste ⓕ post
make-up maquillage ⓜ ma·kee·yazh
man homme ⓜ om
manager (restaurant, hotel)
gérant(e) ⓜ/ⓕ zhay·ron(t)
map (of country) carte ⓕ kart
map (of town) plan ⓜ plon
market marché ⓜ mar·shay
meal repas ⓜ rer·pa
meat viande ⓕ vyond
medicine (medication) médicament
ⓜ may·dee·ka·mon
metro station station ⓕ de métro

sta·syon der may·tro
midday midi mee·dee
midnight minuit mee·nwee
milk lait ⓜ lay
mineral water eau ⓕ minérale o
mee·nay·ral
mobile phone téléphone ⓜ portable
tay·lay·fon por·ta·bler
modem modem ⓜ mo·dem
money argent ⓜ ar·zhon
month mois ⓜ mwa
morning matin ⓜ ma·tun
mother mère ⓕ mair
motorcycle moto ⓕ mo·to
motorway (tollway) autoroute ⓕ
o·to·root
mountain montagne ⓕ mon·ta·nyer
museum musée ⓕ mew·zay
music shop disquaire ⓕ dee·skair

- n -

name nom ⓜ nom
napkin serviette ⓕ sair·vyet
nappy (diaper) couche ⓕ koosh
newsagent marchand ⓜ de journaux
mar·shon der zhoor·no
newspaper journal ⓜ zhoor·nal
next (month) prochain(e) ⓜ/ⓕ
pro·shun/pro·shen
night nuit ⓕ nwee
night out soirée ⓕ swa·ray
nightclub boîte ⓕ bwat
no vacancy complet kom·play
nonsmoking non-fumeur non·few·mer
noon midi mee·dee
north nord ⓜ nor
now maintenant mun·ter·non
number numéro ⓜ new·may·ro

- o -

oil huile ⓕ weel

oil (petrol) pétrole ⓜ pay·trol
one-way (ticket) (billet) simple
(bee·yay) sum·pler
open ouvert(e) ⓜ/ⓕ oo·vair(t)
opening hours heures ⓕ pl
d'ouverture lay zer doo·vair·tewr
orange (colour, fruit) orange o·ronzh

- p -

painter peintre ⓜ pun·trer
painting (a work) tableau ⓜ ta·blo
painting (the art) peinture ⓕ
pun·tewr
pants pantalon ⓜ pon·ta·lon
pantyhose collant ⓜ ko·lon
paper papier ⓜ pa·pyay
party (night out) soirée ⓕ swa·ray
passenger voyageur/voyageuse ⓜ/ⓕ
vwa·ya·zher/vwa·ya·zherz
passport passeport ⓜ pas·por
passport number numéro ⓜ de
passeport new·may·ro der pas·por
path chemin ⓜ shmun
penknife canif ⓜ ka·neef
pensioner retraité(e) ⓜ/ⓕ
rer·tray·tay
petrol essence ⓕ e·sons
petrol station station-service ⓕ
sta·syon·sair·vees
phone book annuaire ⓜ an·wair
phone box cabine ⓕ téléphonique
ka·been tay·lay·fo·neek
phone card télécarte ⓕ tay·lay·kart
phrasebook recueil ⓜ d'expressions
rer·ker·yer dek·spray·syon
picnic pique-nique ⓜ peek·neek
pillow oreiller ⓜ o·ray·yay
pillowcase taie ⓕ d'oreiller tay
do·ray·yay
platform quai ⓜ kay
play (theatre) pièce ⓕ de théâtre
pyes der tay·a·trer
police officer (in city) policier ⓜ

po·lee·syay
police officer (in country)
gendarme ⓜ zhon·darm
police station commissariat ⓜ
ko·mee·sar·ya
post code code ⓜ postal kod pos·tal
post office bureau ⓜ de poste bew·ro
der post
postcard carte postale ⓕ kart
pos·tal
pound (money, weight) livre ⓕ
leev·rer
prescription ordonnance ⓕ
or·do·nons
present (gift) cadeau ⓜ ka·do
price prix ⓜ pree

~ q ~

quiet tranquille trong·keel

~ r ~

receipt reçu ⓜ rer·sew
refund remboursement ⓜ
rom·boor·ser·mon
rent louer loo·ay
repair réparer ray·pa·ray
return revenir rerv·neer
return (ticket) aller retour ⓜ a·lay
rer·toor
road route ⓕ root
room chambre ⓕ shom·brer
room number numéro ⓜ de chambre
new·may·ro der shom·brer

~ s ~

safe coffre-fort ⓜ kof·rer·for
sea mer ⓕ mair
season saison ⓕ say·zon
seat (place) place ⓕ plas
seatbelt ceinture ⓕ de sécurité

sun·tewr der say·kew·ree·tay
self service libre-service ⓜ
lee·brer·sair·vees
service service ⓜ sair·vees
service charge service ⓜ sair·vees
share (a dorm etc) partager
par·ta·zhay
share with partager avec par·ta·zhay
a·vek
shirt chemise ⓕ sher·meez
shoe chaussure ⓕ sho·sewr
shop magasin ⓜ ma·ga·zun
shopping centre centre ⓜ
commercial son·trer ko·mair·syal
short (height) court(e) ⓜ/ⓕ koor(t)
show montrer mon·tray
shower douche ⓕ doosh
sick malade ma·lad
silk soie ⓕ swa
silver argent ⓜ ar·zhon
single (person) célibataire
say·lee·ba·tair
single room chambre ⓕ pour
une personne shom·brer poor ewn
pair·son
sister sœur ⓕ ser
size (general) taille ⓕ tai
skirt jupe ⓕ zhewp
sleeping bag sac ⓜ de couchage sak
der koo·shazh
sleeping car wagon-lit ⓜ va·gon·lee
slide (film) diapositive ⓕ
dya·po·zee·teev
smoke fumée ⓕ few·may
snack casse-croûte ⓜ kas·kroot
snow neige ⓕ nezh
socks chaussettes ⓕ sho·set
son fils ⓜ fees
soon bientôt byun·to
south sud ⓜ sewd
spring (season) printemps ⓜ
prun·tom
square (town) place ⓕ plas
stairway escalier ⓜ es·ka·lyay

ENGLISH *to* FRENCH

81

stamp timbre ⓜ tum·brer
stationer's (shop) papeterie ⓕ pa·pet·ree
stolen volé(e) ⓜ/ⓕ vo·lay
street rue ⓕ rew
student étudiant(e) ⓜ/ⓕ ay·tew·dyon(t)
subtitles sous-titres ⓜ soo·tee·trer
suitcase valise ⓕ va·leez
summer été ⓜ ay·tay
supermarket supermarché ⓜ sew·pair·mar·shay
surface mail (land) voie de terre vwa der tair
surface mail (sea) voie maritime vwa ma·ree·teem
surname nom ⓜ de famille nom der fa·mee·yer
sweater pull ⓜ pewl
swim nager na·zhay
swimming pool piscine ⓕ pee·seen

- t -

taxi stand station ⓕ de taxi sta·syon der tak·see
ticket billet ⓜ bee·yay
ticket machine distributeur ⓜ de tickets dee·stree·bew·ter der tee·kay
ticket office guichet ⓜ gee·shay
time temps ⓜ tom
timetable horaire ⓜ o·rair
tip (gratuity) pourboire ⓜ poor·bwar
to à a
today aujourd'hui o·zhoor·dwee
together ensemble on·som·bler
tomorrow demain der·mun
tour voyage ⓜ vwa·yazh
tourist office office de tourisme ⓜ o·fees·der too·rees·mer
towel serviette ⓕ sair·vyet
train station gare ⓕ gar
transit lounge salle ⓕ de transit sal der tron·zeet
travel agency agence ⓕ de voyage a·zhons der vwa·yazh
travellers cheque chèque ⓜ de voyage shek der vwa·yazh
trousers pantalon ⓜ pon·ta·lon
twin beds lits ⓜ pl jumeaux lee zhew·mo

- u -

underwear sous-vêtements ⓜ soo·vet·mon
urgent urgent(e) ⓜ/ⓕ ewr·zhon(t)

- v -

vacancy chambre ⓕ libre shom·brer lee·brer
vacant libre lee·brer
vacation vacances ⓕ pl va·kons
validate valider va·lee·day
vegetable légume ⓜ lay·gewm
view vue ⓕ vew

- w -

waiting room salle ⓕ d'attente sal da·tont
walk marcher mar·shay
warm chaud(e) ⓜ/ⓕ sho(d)
wash (something) laver la·vay
washing machine machine ⓕ à laver ma·sheen a la·vay
watch montre ⓕ mon·trer
water eau ⓕ o
week semaine ⓕ ser·men
west ouest ⓜ west
when quand kon
where où oo
which quel(le) ⓜ/ⓕ kel
which qui kee
white blanc/blanche ⓜ/ⓕ blong/

blonsh

who qui kee
why pourquoi poor·kwa
wife femme ① fam
window fenêtre ① fer·nay·trer
wine vin ⓜ vun
winter hiver ⓜ ee·vair
without sans son
woman femme ① fam
wool laine ① len

~y~

year année ⓜ a·nay
yes oui wee
yesterday hier ee·yair
you sg inf tu tew
you sg pol & pl vous voo
youth hostel auberge ① de jeunesse
o·bairzh der zher·nes

Dictionary

FRENCH *to* ENGLISH

français – anglais

Nouns in this dictionary have their gender indicated by ⓜ or ⓕ.
If it's a plural noun, you'll also see pl. Where a word that could be
either a noun or a verb has no gender indicated, it's a verb.

~ a ~

à a at • to
addition ⓕ a·dee·syon bill • check
aéroport ⓜ a·ay·ro·por airport
affaires ⓕ a·fair business
agence ⓕ **de voyage** a·zhons der
vwa·yazh travel agency
agence ⓕ **immobilière** a·zhons
ee·mo·bee·lyair estate agency
aider ay·day help
alcool ⓜ al·kol alcohol
aller a·lay go
aller et retour ⓜ a·lay ay rer·toor
return (ticket)
ambassade ⓕ om·ba·sad embassy
amende ⓕ a·mond fine (penalty)
ami(e) ⓜ/ⓕ a·mee friend
anglais(e) ⓜ/ⓕ ong·glay(z) English

année ⓜ a·nay year
anniversaire ⓜ a·nee·vair·sair
birthday
annuaire ⓜ an·wair phone book
annuler a·new·lay cancel
antiquité ⓕ on·tee·kee·tay antique
appareil ⓜ **photo** a·pa·ray fo·to
camera
appeler a·play call
après-demain a·pray·der·mun day
after tomorrow
après-midi ⓜ a·pray·mee·dee
afternoon
argent ⓜ ar·zhon cash • money •
silver
arrêt ⓜ **d'autobus** a·ray do·to·bews
bus stop
arrivées ⓕ a·ree·vay arrivals
artisanat ⓜ ar·tee·za·na crafts

ascenseur ⓜ a·son·ser elevator • lift
assez a·say enough
assurance ⓕ a·sew·rons insurance
Attention! a·ton·syon Careful!
auberge ⓕ **de jeunesse** o·bairzh der zher·nes youth hostel
aujourd'hui o·zhoor·dwee today
auto ⓜ o·to car
automne ⓜ o·ton autumn • fall
autoroute ⓕ o·to·root highway • motorway
avant-hier a·von·tyair day before yesterday
avion ⓜ a·vyon aeroplane

~ b ~

bac ⓜ bak ferry
bagages ⓜ pl ba·gazh baggage • luggage
baignoire ⓕ be·nywar bath
banque ⓕ bongk bank
bateau ⓜ ba·to boat
bâtiment ⓜ ba·tee·mon building
beau/belle ⓜ/ⓕ bo/bel beautiful • handsome
bébé ⓜ bay·bay baby
bientôt byun·to soon
bière ⓕ byair beer
bijoux ⓜ pl bee·zhoo jewellery
billet ⓜ bee·yay ticket
— simple sum·pler one-way ticket
blanc/blanche ⓜ/ⓕ blong/blonsh white
bleu(e) ⓜ/ⓕ bler blue
boire bwar drink
boisson ⓕ bwa·son drink (beverage)
boîte ⓕ bwat box • can (tin) • carton (for ice cream) • nightclub
boucherie ⓕ boosh·ree butcher's shop
boulangerie ⓕ boo·lon·zhree bakery
bouteille ⓕ boo·tay bottle
briquet ⓜ bree·kay cigarette lighter
brun/brune ⓜ/ⓕ brun/brewn brown

bureau ⓜ bew·ro office
— de poste der post post office
— des objets trouvés day zob·zhay troo·vay lost property office
bus ⓜ bews bus (city)

~ c ~

cabine ⓕ **téléphonique** ka·been tay·lay·fo·neek phone box
cadeau ka·do gift • present
café ka·fay cafe • coffee
caissier/caissière ⓜ/ⓕ kay·syay/kay·syair cashier • teller
campagne ⓕ kom·pa·nyer countryside
canif ⓜ ka·neef penknife
car ⓜ kar bus (intercity)
carte ⓕ kart map (of country)
— de crédit kart der kray·dee credit card
— d'embarquement kart dom·bar·ker·mon boarding pass
— d'identité kart dee·don·tee·tay identification card (ID)
— grise kart greez car owner's title
— postale kart pos·tal postcard
cassé(e) ⓜ/ⓕ ka·say broken
casse-croûte ⓜ kas·kroot snack
ceinture ⓕ **de sécurité** sun·tewr der say·kew·ree·tay seatbelt
célibataire say·lee·ba·tair single (person)
cendrier ⓜ son·dree·yay ashtray
centre ⓜ **commercial** son·trer ko·mair·syal shopping centre
centre-ville ⓜ son·trer·veel city centre
chambre ⓕ shom·brer room
— à coucher a koo·shay bedroom
— libre lee·brer vacancy
— pour deux personnes poor der pair·son double room
— pour une personne poor ewn pair·son single room
changer shon·zhay change
chaque shak each • every

chaud(e) ⓜ/ⓕ show(d) hot • warm
chauffé(e) ⓜ/ⓕ sho·fay heated
chaussettes ⓕ sho·set socks
chaussure ⓕ sho·sewr shoe
chemin ⓜ shmun path • lane • way
chemise ⓕ sher·meez shirt
chèque ⓜ shek check (banking) • cheque
— de voyage der vwa·yazh travellers cheque
cher/chère ⓜ/ⓕ shair expensive • dear
chercher shair·shay look for
chien ⓜ shyun dog
cimetière ⓕ seem·tyair cemetery
cirque ⓜ seerk circus
classe affaires ⓕ klas a·fair business class
classe touriste ⓕ klas too·reest economy class
clé ⓕ klay key
climatisé kee·ma·tee·zay air-conditioned
code ⓜ **postal** kod pos·tal post code
coffre-fort ⓜ kof·rer·for safe
collant ⓜ ko·lon pantyhose
commissariat ⓜ ko·mee·sar·ya police station
complet/complète ⓜ/ⓕ kom·play/ kom·plet booked up • no vacancy
compris(e) ⓜ/ⓕ kom·pree(z) included
compte ⓜ kont account
— bancaire bong·kair bank account
confirmer kon·feer·may confirm (a booking)
confortable kon·for·ta·bler comfortable
consigne ⓕ kon·see·nyer left luggage (office)
— automatique o·to·ma·teek luggage lockers
couche ⓕ koosh diaper • nappy
court(e) ⓜ/ⓕ koor(t) short (height)
couvert ⓜ koo·vair cover charge
couverture ⓕ koo·vair·tewr blanket
cuir ⓜ kweer leather

cuisine ⓕ kwee·zeen kitchen
cuisinier/cuisinière ⓜ/ⓕ kwee·zee·nyay/kwee·zee·nyair cook
cybercafé ⓜ see·bair·ka·fay internet cafe

-d-

date ⓕ **de naissance** dat der nay·sons date of birth
déjeuner ⓜ day·zher·nay lunch
demain der·mun tomorrow
— après-midi a·pray·mee·dee tomorrow afternoon
— matin ma·tun tomorrow morning
— soir swar tomorrow evening
départ ⓜ day·par departure
dépôt ⓜ day·po deposit
dernier/dernière ⓜ/ⓕ dair·nyay/ dair·nyair last (previous)
diapositive ⓕ dya·po·zee·teev slide (film)
dictionnaire ⓜ deek·syo·nair dictionary
dîner ⓜ dee·nay dinner
direct(e) ⓜ/ⓕ dee·rekt direct
disquaire ⓜ dee·skair music shop
distributeur ⓜ **de tickets** dee·stree·bew·ter der tee·kay ticket machine
doigt ⓜ dwa finger
dos ⓜ do back (body)
douane ⓕ dwan customs
douche ⓕ doosh shower
draps ⓜ dra bed linen

-e-

eau ⓕ o water
— minérale mee·nay·ral mineral water
échange ⓜ ay·shonzh exchange
échanger ay·shon·zhay change (money) • exchange
église ⓕ ay·gleez church

en retard on rer·tar late
enfant ⓜ&ⓕ on·fon child
enregistrement
on·rer·zhee·strer·mon check-in (desk)
ensemble on·som·bler together
entracte ⓜ on·trakt intermission
entrée ⓕ on·tray entry
entreprise ⓕ on·trer·preez company
enveloppe ⓕ on·vlop envelope
épicerie ⓕ ay·pee·sree grocery
escalier ⓜ es·ka·lyay stairway
essence ⓕ ay·sons gas • petrol
est ⓜ est east
étage ⓜ ay·tazh floor (storey)
été ⓜ ay·tay summer
étranger/étrangère ⓜ/ⓕ
ay·tron·zhay/ay·tron·zhair foreign •
stranger
étudiant(e) ⓜ/ⓕ ay·tew·dyon(t)
student
excédent ek·say·don excess
(baggage)
exposition ⓕ ek·spo·zee·syon
exhibition
exprès eks·pres express (mail)

- f -

faire les courses fair lay koors go
shopping
famille ⓕ fa·mee·yer family
félicitations fay·lee·see·ta·syon
congratulations
femme ⓕ fam wife • woman
fenêtre ⓕ fer·nay·trer window
fermé(e) ⓜ/ⓕ fair·may closed
— à clé a klay locked
fièvre ⓕ fyev·rer fever
fille ⓕ fee·yer daughter • girl
fils ⓜ fees son
forêt ⓕ fo·ray forest
frais/fraîche ⓜ/ⓕ fray/fresh cool •
fresh
franchise ⓕ fron·sheez baggage
allowance
freins ⓜ frun brakes

frère ⓜ frair brother
froid(e) ⓜ/ⓕ frwa(d) cold
frontière ⓕ fron·tyair border
fumer few·may smoke

- g -

gants ⓜ pl gon gloves
garçon ⓜ gar·son boy
gare ⓕ gar train station
— routière roo·tyair bus station
gaz ⓜ gaz gas (for cooking)
gendarme ⓜ zhon·darm police
officer (in country)
gentil(le) ⓜ/ⓕ zhon·tee kind • nice
gérant(e) ⓜ/ⓕ zhay·ron(t) manager
(restaurant, hotel)
grand(e) ⓜ/ⓕ gron(d) big • large •
tall
grand lit ⓜ gron lee double bed
grand magasin ⓜ gron ma·ga·zun
department store
gratuit(e) ⓜ/ⓕ gra·twee(t) free
(gratis)
grippe ⓕ greep flu
gris(e) ⓜ/ⓕ gree(z) gray • grey
groupe ⓜ **sanguin** groop song·gun
blood group
guichet ⓜ gee·shay ticket office
— automatique de banque (GAB)
o·to·ma·teek der bonk ATM

- h -

heure ⓕ er hour • time
heures ⓕ pl **d'ouverture** er
doo·vair·tewr opening hours
hier ee·yair yesterday
hiver ⓜ ee·vair winter
homme ⓜ om man
hôpital ⓜ o·pee·tal hospital
horaire ⓜ o·rair timetable
hors service or sair·vees out of order
hôtel ⓜ o·tel hotel
huile ⓕ weel oil

- i -

ici ee·see here
immatriculation
ee·ma·tree·kew·la·syon car
registration
interprète ⓜ/ⓕ un·tair·pret
interpreter
itinéraire ⓜ ee·tee·nay·rair itinerary •
route
ivre ee·vrer drunk

- j -

jardin ⓜ zhar·dun garden
jean ⓜ zheen jeans
jour ⓜ zhoor day
journal ⓜ zhoor·nal newspaper
jupe ⓕ zhewp skirt

- l -

laine ⓕ len wool
lait ⓜ lay milk
laver la·vay wash (something)
laverie ⓕ lav·ree launderette
légume ⓜ lay·gewm vegetable
lettre ⓕ lay·trer letter
librairie ⓕ lee·bray·ree bookshop
libre lee·brer free (at liberty) •
vacant
libre-service ⓜ lee·brer·sair·vees
self service
lin ⓜ lun linen (material)
linge ⓜ lunzh laundry (clothes) •
linen
lit ⓜ lee bed
lits ⓜ pl **jumeaux** lee zhew·mo twin
beds
livre ⓜ leev·rer book
livre ⓕ leev·rer pound (money,
weight)
location ⓕ **de voitures** lo·ka·syon
der vwa·tewr car hire
logement ⓜ lozh·mon

accommodation
louer loo·ay hire • rent
lune ⓕ **de miel** lewn der myel
honeymoon
lunettes ⓕ pl lew·net glasses
(spectacles)

- m -

machine ⓕ **à laver** ma·sheen a la·vay
washing machine
magasin ⓜ ma·ga·zun shop
magnétoscope ⓜ ma·nyay·to·skop
video recorder
maintenant mun·ter·non now
malade ma·lad ill • sick
manger mon·zhay eat
manteau ⓜ mon·to coat
maquillage ⓜ ma·kee·yazh
make-up
marchand de journaux ⓜ mar·shon
der zhoor·no newsagent
marché ⓜ mar·shay market
— aux puces o pews fleamarket
marcher mar·shay walk
mari ⓜ ma·ree husband
matin ⓜ ma·tun morning
mauvais(e) ⓜ/ⓕ mo·vay(z) bad •
off (meat) • wrong (direction)
médecin ⓜ mayd·sun doctor
médicament ⓜ may·dee·ka·mon
medicine (medication)
mer ⓕ mair sea
mère ⓕ mair mother
midi ⓜ mee·dee midday • noon
minuit ⓜ mee·nwee midnight
mode ⓕ mod fashion
mois ⓜ mwa month
moitié ⓕ mwa·tyay half
monnaie ⓕ mo·nay change (coins)
montagne ⓕ mon·ta·nyer
mountain
montre ⓕ mon·trer watch
moto ⓕ mo·to motorcycle
musée ⓜ mew·zay art gallery •
museum

- n -

nager na·zhay swim
neige ① nezh snow
nettoyage ⓜ net·wa·yazh cleaning
nettoyer net·wa·yay clean
Noël ⓜ no·el Christmas
noir(e) ⓜ/① nwar black
noir et blanc nwar ay blong B&W
(film)
nom ⓜ nom name
— de famille der fa·mee·yer surname
non-fumeur non·few·mer nonsmoking
nord ⓜ nor north
nuit ① nwee night
numéro ⓜ new·may·ro number
— de chambre der shom·brer room
number
— de passeport der pas·por passport
number

- o -

occupé(e) ⓜ/① o·kew·pay busy
office de tourisme ⓜ o·fees·der
too·rees·mer tourist office
or ⓜ or gold
orange o·ronzh orange (colour, fruit)
ordinateur ⓜ or·dee·na·ter
computer
— portable por·ta·bler laptop
ordonnance ① or·do·nons
prescription
oreiller ⓜ o·ray·yay pillow
où oo where
ouest ⓜ west west
ouvert(e) ⓜ/① oo·vair(t) open

- p -

pain ⓜ pun bread
palais ⓜ pa·lay palace
pantalon ⓜ pon·ta·lon pants •
trousers

papeterie ① pa·pet·ree stationer's
(shop)
papier ⓜ pa·pyay paper
partager par·ta·zhay share
partir par·teer depart • leave
passeport ⓜ pas·por passport
peintre ⓜ pun·trer painter
peinture ① pun·tewr painting (the
art)
pellicule ① pay·lee·kewl film (for
camera)
pension ① pon·syon boarding house •
bed & breakfast
— de famille der fa·mee·yer
guesthouse
perdu(e) ⓜ/① pair·dew lost
père ⓜ pair father
permis de conduire ⓜ pair·mee der
kon·dweer drivers licence
petit ami ⓜ per·tee a·mee boyfriend
petite ami ① per·teet a·mee
girlfriend
pièce de théâtre pyes der
tay·a·trer play (theatre)
pièce ① d'identité pyes
dee·don·tee·tay identification
pièces ① pyes coins
pile ① peel battery
pique-nique ⓜ peek·neek picnic
piscine ① pee·seen swimming pool
place ① plas seat (place) • square
(town)
plage ① plazh beach
plan ⓜ plon map (of town)
plat ⓜ pla dish
plus tard plew·tar later
poissonnerie ① pwa·son·ree fish
shop
policier ⓜ po·lee·syay police officer
(in city)
poste ① post mail (postal system)
pourboire ⓜ poor·bwar tip
(gratuity)
pourquoi poor·kwa why
première classe ① prer·myair klas
first class

prénom ⓜ pray·non first name
préservatif ⓜ pray·zair·va·teef condom
printemps ⓜ prun·tom spring (season)
prix ⓜ pree price
prochain(e) ⓜ/ⓕ pro·shun/pro·shen next (month)
pull ⓜ pewl jumper • sweater

- q -

quai ⓜ kay platform
quand kon when
quel/quelle ⓜ/ⓕ kel what • which
qui kee which • who
quotidien(ne) ⓜ/ⓕ ko·tee·dyun/ ko·tee·dyen daily

- r -

rapide ra·peed fast • quick
rapport ⓜ ra·por connection
reconnaissant(e) ⓜ/ⓕ rer·ko·nay·son(t) grateful
reçu ⓜ rer·sew receipt
recueil d'expressions rer·ker·yer dek·spray·syon phrasebook
remboursement ⓜ rom·boor·ser·mon refund
remise ⓕ rer·meez discount
rendez-vous ⓜ ron·day·voo appointment • date
renseignements ⓜ pl ron·sen·yer·mon information
réparer ray·pa·ray repair
repas ⓜ rer·pa meal
réserver ray·zair·vay book (make a booking)
retard ⓜ rer·tar delay
retrait des bagages rer·tray day ba·gazh baggage claim
retraité(e) ⓜ/ⓕ rer·tray·tay pensioner • retired
réveil ⓜ ray·vay alarm clock

revenir rerv·neer return
robe ⓕ rob dress
rose roz pink
rouge roozh red
route ⓕ root road
rue ⓕ rew street

- s -

sac ⓜ sak bag
— à dos a do a backpack
— de couchage der koo·shazh sleeping bag
saison ⓕ say·zon season
sale sal dirty
salle ⓕ sal room
— d'attente sal da·tont waiting room
— de bain sal der bun bathroom
— de transit sal der tron·zeet transit lounge
salon de beauté sa·lon der bo·tay beauty salon
sans son without
sec/sèche ⓜ/ⓕ sek/sesh dry
semaine ⓕ ser·men week
sentier ⓜ son·tyay footpath
service ⓜ sair·vees service • service charge
serviette ⓕ sair·vyet briefcase • napkin • towel
sœur ⓕ ser sister
soie ⓕ swa silk
soir ⓜ swar evening
soirée ⓕ swa·ray night out • party
sortie ⓕ sor·tee exit
sortir sor·teer go out
sous-titres ⓜ soo·tee·trer subtitles
sous-vêtements ⓜ soo·vet·mon underwear
soutien-gorge ⓜ soo·tyung·gorzh bra
sparadrap ⓜ spa·ra·dra Band-Aid
spectacle ⓜ spek·ta·kler performance • show

station ① **de métro** sta·syon der may·tro metro station

station ① **de taxi** sta·syon der tak·see taxi stand

station-service ① sta·syon·sair·vees petrol station

sud ⓜ sewd south

supérette ① **de quartier** sew·pay·ret der kar·tyay convenience store

supermarché ⓜ sew·pair·mar·shay supermarket

~ t ~

tableau ⓜ ta·blo painting (a work)

taie ① **d'oreiller** tay do·ray·yay pillowcase

taille ① tai size (general)

tailleur ⓜ ta·yer tailor

tante ① tont aunt

tarif ⓜ ta·reef fare

taux ⓜ **de change** to der shonzh currency exchange

taxe ① **d'aéroport** taks da·ay·ro·por airport tax

télécarte ① tay·lay·kart phone card

téléphone ⓜ **portable** tay·lay·fon por·ta·bler mobile phone

télésiège ⓜ tay·lay·syezh chairlift (skiing)

timbre ⓜ tum·brer stamp

tôt to early

tout(e) ⓜ/① too(t) everything

toux ① too cough

traiteur ⓜ tre·ter delicatessen

~ v ~

vacances ① pl va·kons holidays • vacation

valider va·lee·day validate

valise ① va·leez suitcase

vélo ⓜ vay·lo bicycle

vert(e) ⓜ/① vair(t) green

veste ① vest jacket

vestiaire ⓜ vays·tyair cloakroom

vêtements ⓜ vet·mon clothing

viande ① vyond meat

ville ① veel city • town

vin ⓜ vun wine

visite ① **guidée** vee·zeet gee·day guided tour

voie de terre vw der tair surface mail (land)

voie maritime vwa ma·ree·teem surface mail (sea)

voiture ① vwa·tewr car

vol ⓜ vol flight • robbery

volé(e) ⓜ/① vo·lay stolen

voyage ⓜ vwa·yazh journey • tour • trip

— d'affaires da·fair business trip

voyageur/voyageuse ⓜ/① vwa·ya·zher/vwa·ya·zherz passenger

vue ① vew view

~ w ~

wagon-lit ⓜ va·gon·lee sleeping car

wagon-restaurant ⓜ va·gon·res·to·ron dining car

Acknowledgments
Associate Product Director Angela Tinson
Product Editor Kathryn Rowan
Language Writers Michael Janes, Jean-Pierre Masclef, Jean-Bernard Carillet
Cover Designer Campbell McKenzie

Thanks
Kate Chapman, Gwen Cotter, James Hardy, Indra Kilfoyle, Wibowo Rusli, Juan Winata

Published by Lonely Planet Global Ltd
CRN 554153

4th Edition – June 2018
Text © Lonely Planet 2018
Cover Image Paris, France – Jan Christopher Becke/AWL ©

Printed in China 10 9 8 7 6 5 4 3 2

Contact lonelyplanet.com/contact

MIX
Paper from
responsible sources
FSC™ C021741

Index

10. Phrases to Get You Talking

Hello.	Bonjour. bon·zhoor
Goodbye.	Au revoir. o rer·vwar
Please.	S'il vous plaît. seel voo play
Thank you.	Merci. mair·see
Excuse me.	Excusez-moi. ek·skew·zay·mwa
Sorry.	Pardon. par·don
Yes.	Oui. wee
No.	Non. non
I don't understand.	Je ne comprends pas. zher ner kom·pron pa
How much is it?	C'est combien? say kom·byun